Ruth Etchells is a distinguished lbined the study of English literatu
her life. After teaching at a gram
then training teachers at Chester College, she moved to university work in Durham in 1968. She founded the university course there in theology and literature while serving as Vice-Principal of Trevelyan College. In 1978 she was appointed Principal of St John's College. This university college also includes a theological training hall (Cranmer Hall), and so she became the first lay person and the first woman to be the head of a Church of England theological college.

After her retirement from university work, she continued to serve widely in the Church, including on the General Synod, the Doctrine Commission and the Crown Appointments Commission. She remains much involved in local Christian life, particularly in Durham Cathedral. Her books include *Unafraid to Be* (1968), *Set My People Free* (Archbishop's Lent Book, 1996) and *Just As I Am* (1994), the predecessor of *Safer than a Known Way* (2006). The Archbishop of Canterbury conferred on her the Lambeth DD in 1992 for 'services to education, theological scholarship, and the work of the General Synod', and in 2003, during its 100th birthday celebrations, the University of Liverpool made her an Hon. Litt.D.

A RAINBOW-COLOURED CROSS

PERSONAL PRAYERS WITH EASTER SUPPLEMENT

RUTH ETCHELLS

First published in Great Britain in 2007

Society for Promoting Christian Knowledge
36 Causton Street
London SW1P 4ST

British Library Cataloguing-in-Publication Data
A catalogue record for this book is available from the British Library

ISBN-13: 978–0–281–05786–3
ISBN-10: 0–281–05786–9

1 3 5 7 9 10 8 6 4 2

Typeset in 11/13.5pt Minion by Graphicraft Limited, Hong Kong
Printed in Great Britain by Bookmarque Ltd, Croydon, Surrey

*For the worshipping community at Durham Cathedral
with my deep gratitude for the (nearly!) 40 years of
our shared prayer.*

> *Cathedrals . . . learn from trees*
> *The branching vault, and canopies*
> *Of fretted space. The ecstasy*
> *Of power is here, coiled like a spring,*
> *A god's mysterious gaiety,*
> *And peace that passes understanding.*
> *And this is home to us.*
>
> *Anne Ridler*[1]

Contents

SEASONAL SUPPLEMENT FOR LENT, PALM SUNDAY, HOLY WEEK, EASTER, ASCENSION DAY, PENTECOST AND TRINITY SUNDAY

Introduction

Prayer has always been a bridge between the mundane and the holy, reminding us that the Earth is hallowed ground and all our daily doings the subject of God's love. But sometimes we need to remind ourselves, too, that it is the transcendent to which we are opening ourselves, and its power is immeasurable, and beyond our conceiving.

Sometimes a comment about what prayer has meant to someone in extreme conditions challenges all one's comfortable devotional habits and the limited expectations thereof. Recently I read an account about what prayer had meant to a Russian dissident who had suffered in the horrors of the twentieth-century purges in Russia. He wrote:

> The greatest miracle of all is prayer. I have only to turn my thoughts to God and I suddenly feel a force bursting into me; there is a new strength in my soul, in my entire being . . . The basis of my whole spiritual life is the Orthodox liturgy, so while I was in prison I attended it every day in my imagination . . . I would begin praying in my own words, remembering all those near to me, those in prison and those who were free, those still alive and those who had died . . . The prison walls moved apart and the whole universe became my residence, visible and invisible, the universe for which that wounded, pierced body offered itself as a sacrifice . . .
>
> Not only my own prayer helped me, but even more the prayer of many other faithful Christians. I felt it continually, working from a distance, lifting me up as though on wings, giving me living water and the bread of life, peace of soul, rest and love.[2]

'The prison walls moved apart.' What a wonder, even in our ordinary dailiness, to recover this experience of the extraordinary power we can call upon that is available to us through prayer. And available through us, for others, if we will remember them before God. The Lord is transcendent as well as incarnate, and so our prayer to him bridges the visible and invisible worlds, which are alike under his sovereignty.

It is this experience that underlies the very personal prayers in this book, morning and evening for a month. They are part of a daily dialogue with that same Lord, catching moments of his glory, struggling with the obduracy of ordinary life, wrestling with his seeming absence, and rejoicing in his presence, whether in the small tasks of the everyday or in those moments of exaltation when, like the prophet Isaiah, we too see the Lord high and lifted up, and know him for the Most Holy One. We may come to the prayer for the day to find it glorying when our own current experience is of the absent God – or vice versa. I have found that I can use such disjunctions to remind me of the times when I have felt otherwise, and so offer up the whole of my life, not just the current dominating moment. And this helps us to gather up others also in our prayers, whose current situation may be very different from our own.

This is a companion book to its predecessor, *Safer than a Known Way*, and just as that offered a Seasonal Supplement (of prayers for Advent, Christmas and Epiphany) so this similarly offers seasonal prayers, for Lent, Holy Week, Easter, Ascension Day, Pentecost and Trinity Sunday. These supplementary prayers, too, are personal, though in some cases adaptable for public prayer: they are personal reflections on the journey from Ash Wednesday to Trinity Sunday.

I have also included, as in that first volume, some of the most requested prayers from *Just As I Am*, an initial volume of prayers now out of print.

As I conclude these two volumes I find myself turning again to that extraordinary testimony of the former Russian prisoner. Out of his own profound experience he was affirming that prayer is a key that unlocks prison gates and frees us into this world and the next. My longing is that in some way the prayers in these two books will help to do just that, releasing us from whatever binds or imprisons us and narrows our existence, that we may discover for ourselves again the marvellous liberty that is God's gift; and so enter more fully into our inheritance.

Grateful thanks

These two volumes of prayer, because they were slow-growing fruit, owe their appearance – at last! – both to people in the immediate present and to others over a number of years.

Thanks are therefore due to SPCK, especially Alison Barr, Senior Editor, and Louise Clairmonte, Editorial Manager, for their warm support, encouragement and detailed care of the text and its presentation (and for their patience!).

To some beloved friends: Anne Harrison, for her unfailing and eager interest and support, not least in retrieving for me certain sought-after sources; and Jamie Harrison, for his timely interventions through action and through generous word, when difficulties beyond the work could have been seriously distracting (and not least for staying me with flagons . . .); and Pauline Pepper, for her personal desire that these books should happen, and for keeping my home running while they did.

To the many others who over the years have asked for these books, and helped pray them into existence. And specially to David Kennedy, friend and Spiritual Director, who shared the life out of which these prayers have grown.

And finally, to my earliest guide in Christ, and dear fellow pilgrim through the decades, Mally Yates, who first – some fifty years ago – drew me into the wonder, power and comfort, of personal prayer.

Ruth Etchells
Durham

The cover shows the stained-glass window 'Prodigal Love', designed and made by Ruth Etchells for the Leech Hall, St John's College, University of Durham. Reproduced by kind permission of the Principal.

Days

First Day • MORNING

I was made for this green planet
This tight ball
Of infinite beauty
Alive with the possibilities
Of his creative power . . .

I was made to be human
In this most human place.
I was made for Earth:
The Earth is my home.
That's why I'm glad
That God, more than anyone,
Is a Friend of the Earth.
That he was prepared
To die for its restoration.
And that's why I'm glad
That the magnificent, jewelled foundations
Of the mighty Pearly Gates,
Will be anchored
Deeply and for ever
In the soil of Earth.[3]

O Lord, thank you for my place here on your Earth, in your Universe. Help me now and in the days that lie ahead to live faithfully obeying you, Friend of the Earth, whatever life changes that might involve. And all glory to you for the loveliness of our world – even in spite of what we have done to it – and for all the creatures that inhabit it. May this your Creation know your deepest blessing. And keep us creaturely. Amen.

Cathedral builders

They climbed on sketchy ladders towards God,
With winch and pulley hoisted hewn rock into heaven,
Inhabited sky with hammers, defied gravity,
Deified stone, took up God's house to meet Him . . .

Saw naves sprout arches, clerestories soar,
Cursed the loud fancy glaziers for their luck,
Somehow escaped the plague, got rheumatism,
Decided it was time to give it up,

To leave the spire to others; stood in the crowd
Well back from the vestments at the consecration,
Envied the fat bishop his warm boots,
Cocked up a squint eye and said, 'I bloody did that.'[4]

> Slowly the funeral eulogies
> Build up, stone by stone,
> The outline of a life.
> Listening, the wondering spirit,
> Seeing the shape emerging
> Of something far richer than had seemed,
> Marvels, like the medieval builder,
> 'It was I – did that!'

> Then the Master-Builder shows his hands:
> And lo! they are bloody, too . . .

Lord, thank you for the life that is taking shape as I live and
labour from day to day. Keep me true to your design, com-
pliant to your guidance, conscious of your supporting presence;

and grateful for my fellow workers and the help they give me. Hold me faithful even when I am weary, and aware always of your shaping hands redeeming all that I botch. And may the completed building honour you, my Lord. Amen.

Second Day • MORNING

God beyond borders
we bless you for strange places
and different dreams

for the demands and diversity
of a wider world . . .

We bless you
for the friendship of strangers
the richness of other cultures
and the painful gift of freedom

Blessed are you,
God beyond borders.

But if we have overlooked
the exiles in our midst
heightened their exclusion
by our indifference
given our permission
for a climate of fear
and tolerated a culture of violence

Have mercy on us,
God who takes sides with justice,
Confront our prejudice
Stretch our narrowness
Sift out our laws and our lives
with the penetrating insight
of your spirit
until generosity is our only measure.[5]

Lord, I so often delight in the diversity of the world without being prepared to embrace it on my own patch. Give me the courage to work in my nation for a generous acceptance of the alien and the asylum-seeker, recognizing as I share the good things of this society with those crowding to join us, that in sharing my resources with the strangers I share them with you. Amen.

Second Day • EVENING

Have mercy
Upon us.
Have mercy
Upon our efforts,
That we,
Before Thee,
In love and in faith,
Righteousness and humility,
May follow thee,
With self-denial, steadfastness and courage,
And meet Thee
In the silence.

Give us a pure heart
That we may see Thee,
A humble heart
That we may hear Thee,
A heart of love
That we may serve Thee,
A heart of faith
That we may love Thee.[6]

'And meet you in the silence . . .'
So here and now, my Lord, I take silence.

. . .

And in that silence, as I meet you
        It is *your* faith
                    righteousness
                    humility
(and above all) love
that shapes the silence.
Here and now I ponder on them, Lord.
                . . .
O Lord, may I gather them from you
        so that they shape my life as well as my silence;
        my thinking as well as my actions;
        my heart as well as my works;
        what I am to others as well as what I long to be
            for you.
        For your love for the world's sake.
                        Amen.

Third Day • MORNING

And this is my prayer, that your love may overflow more
and more with knowledge and full insight to help you
determine what is best, so that on the day of Jesus Christ
you may be pure and blameless, having produced the
harvest of righteousness that comes through Jesus Christ
. . . Only, live your life in a manner worthy of the gospel of
Christ . . . Do nothing from selfish ambition or conceit . . .
Let the same mind be in you that was in Christ Jesus . . .
who humbled himself . . . and became obedient to the
point of death . . . Therefore . . . work out your own
salvation with fear and trembling.

(Philippians 1.9–2.12)

I don't know what to do, Lord. A lot of the time, I don't know
what to do. Situations are rarely clear-cut, relationships are com-
plex, demands are contradictory, choices are blurred. Which way
to go? For whom give time – energy – money – attention – even
prayer?

And then you send me a letter like this one. And the guide-
lines are there again, never quite obliterated by the drifting
accumulation of time, emerging unmistakably as soon as I look
for them with a proper care.

Your letter reminds me that the way I live my life will always
be shaped by my mind-set; and my heart-set. You remind me
of the simple rule: always to remove myself from the centre of
that mind-set and heart-set. And every time I find I have
wormed my way back into being the focus of my concerns again
(and how quickly and self-justifyingly I do that!) – to *laugh* at
this Gollum-like creature weaselling its way in; and turn back
to the joy of Christ being there instead. And so the heart is

peopled with so many thronging round him, in their need and their love.

But we use the term 'mind-set' rightly, don't we, Lord? For even when heart and soul are centred on you and the others you bring with you, we still need to sort out priorities. And your letter is pretty straight about that, too: 'that your love may overflow more and more with knowledge and full insight'. Why? – 'to help you determine what is best'.

Lord Jesus, help me today and in the days to come to study your Word, and listen to those whom you send as your guides; but also to take every opportunity to gain greater understanding of the human heart, and its preoccupations and needs. That I may love those among whom I live 'with full insight', rather than in some naive, rather ignorant fashion, alert to what is happening in my world and theirs, in the culture we share and the pressure it exerts on us. And beneath all that, humankind itself, your loved and wandering creation, and our potential for nobility and baseness, victory and disaster. Use all such knowledge you can give me to 'determine what is best'.

Dear Lord, the way is clear enough when I let myself face it. But it's a frightening one, because it means becoming obedient to the point of death. Help me, gentle, loving, patient Lord, to be prepared to die to just one little thing today that I don't want to die to. And so begin to pick my way, slowly, down that same road that is yours. And, my Lord, be not just present but sovereign in my heart on that journey. For your love's sake. Amen.

Third Day • EVENING

The apologist's evening prayer

From all my lame defeats and oh! much more
From all the victories I seemed to score;
From cleverness shot forth on Thy behalf
At which, while angels weep, the audience laugh;
From all my proofs of Thy divinity,
Thou, who would'st give no sign, deliver me.
Thoughts are but coins. Let me not trust, instead
Of Thee, their thin-worn image of Thy head.
From all my thoughts,
Even from my thoughts of Thee,
O Thou fair Silence, fall, and set me free.
Lord of the narrow gate and the needle's eye,
Take from me all my trumpery lest I die.[7]

O Lord, save me from cleverly debating theologians (and from trying to be one myself). I listen to the Church's disputes, and, O Lord, I grieve for the energy wasted and the vision lost. Forgive us that we spend so much time defending fragments of disputable territory as though your sovereignty over the whole continent of humankind depended on it. Forgive us that we inflate the importance of this or that issue over the one supreme command, to declare your transforming Love, by all that we do and are, to a world desperate for it.

So today, Lord, I offer you sadly all the matters at dispute in the churches and between the churches. Forgive us, Lord, that we have let them matter too much. Forgive *me*, Lord, that *I* have let them matter too much.

Take my attention and my zeal and fix them on *you*: what do I see and what do you say? I see a Lord who stood between those who condemned and the offender, and refused complicity with either.

> 'Let him that is without sin among you cast the first
> stone' . . . 'Woman . . . has no-one condemned you? . . .
> Neither do I: go now and sin no more'.
>
> *(John 8.7–11, AV)*

I see a Lord who refused to accept the mere cleverness of questions meant not to discover truth but to score points.

> 'Whose is the superscription on this coin? . . . Then render
> to Caesar the things that are Caesar's, and to God the
> things that are God's.'
>
> *(Mark 12.16–17, AV)*

I see a Lord who grieved over religious leaders who cared more about their political standing with the crowds than with examining their hearts to find the truth.

> 'John's baptism: was it from heaven or from men?' And
> they feared the people . . . So they said, 'We cannot tell' . . .
> Then he said, 'Neither will I tell you . . .'
>
> *(Matthew 21.25–27, AV)*

O Lord, sift my heart today that it is purged of the need to win arguments about you for the sake of pride or public or party approval. Give me the wisdom to see the real issue, the issue of God's love, in all the perplexities and problems that the world and religious faith offer. Give me the courage to stand with neither side in human controversy, but to stand between, refusing either judgementalism or compromise with wrong.

O dear Lord Jesus, my world is riven with dispute – small domestic fractiousness, and great issues of faith and behaviour. And you walk among us showing us humour and peaceableness and the larger understanding of Love; and call on us to live, and if necessary die, that your peace may reign here among us. Save me from my own disputatiousness; teach me your silence, your enduring compassion, and your unconditional love. And to you be the glory. Amen.

Fourth Day • MORNING

When all your mercies, O my God,
  My rising soul surveys,
Transported with the view, I'm lost
  In wonder, love and praise.[8]

Sometimes, dear Father God, I am seized by such a profound sense of your love and mercy to me throughout my life. I look back and wonder at the way you have brought me. I look round and marvel at your present provision for me. And I cannot but feel a sense of your personal providence: a wondering conviction that I, small human fragment that I am, am the object of your loving care. And as for me, so for millions through the centuries who have turned to you in fear and hope, and in great thankfulness discovered your grace.

Your servant David has spoken for us:

Then King David went in and sat before the LORD, and said, 'Who am I, O Lord GOD, and what is my house, that you have brought me thus far? . . . O Lord GOD! Because of your promise, and according to your own heart, you have wrought all this . . . so that your servant may know it. Therefore . . . there is no one like you, and there is no God besides you . . . for you, O Lord GOD, have spoken, and with your blessing shall the house of your servant be blessed for ever.'

(from 2 Samuel 7.18–29)

Oh who am I, my Lord God, that you have brought *me* thus far?

And yet, why should it be so great a wonder, when my Lord Jesus Christ, your Son, intervened at such cost twenty centuries ago to transform our human history?

16

Oh who am I that for my sake my Lord should take frail flesh and die?

Help me, my Father God, to understand ever more fully that your loving care for your world *then* is of a piece with your loving care for me *now*: they are woven of the same tender grace, they are shaped by the same energy of loving-kindness, they are a continuum of costliness that your unconditional love undertakes for us.

And so with David I say, you, my Lord God, have spoken; you shape our human histories as we offer them to you; and so, as for me and my house, I affirm with profound thankfulness my trust in your blessing now, and through whatever may lie ahead, for ever.

Almighty God, Father of all mercies, we thine unworthy servants do give thee most humble and hearty thanks for all thy goodness and loving-kindness to us and to all people. We bless thee for our creation, preservation, and all the blessings of this life; but above all for thine inestimable love in the redemption of the world by our Lord Jesus Christ, for the means of grace and for the hope of glory. And we beseech thee, give us that due sense of all thy mercies, that our hearts may be unfeignedly thankful, and that we show forth thy praise, not only with our lips but in our lives; by giving up ourselves to thy service, and by walking before thee in holiness and righteousness all our days; through Jesus Christ our Lord, to whom with thee and the Holy Ghost be all honour and glory, world without end. Amen.[9]

Fourth Day • EVENING

God help my thoughts! they stray from me,
   setting off on the wildest journeys;
When I am at prayer, they run off like naughty
   children, quarrelling, making trouble.
When I read the Bible, they fly to a distant
   place, filled with seductions.
My thoughts can cross an ocean, with a single
   leap; they can fly from earth to heaven, and
   back again, in a single second.
They come to me for a fleeting moment, and
   then away they flee. No chains, no locks
   can hold them back; no threats of punishment
   can restrain them, no hiss of a lash can frighten them.
They slip from my grasp like tails of eels; they
   swoop hither and thither like swallows in flight.
Dear, chaste Christ, who can see into every heart,
   and read every mind, take hold of my thoughts,
   bring my thoughts back to me, and clasp me
   to yourself. Amen.[10]

So, Father, gently gather my flittering thoughts, quietening me
even as a child may be gathered into quietness; so that I may
offer the day's living to you as I long to, trustfully, filled only
with the thought of your loving-kindness as you receive it.

Forgive all wrong in it, Father, and bless all that has been good.
And let me keep heart and thought fixed on you as I ask this:
do not let my soul be caught in the slipstream of my own doings
and thinkings.

Be with those tonight suffering stress or agitation or pain;
and strengthen and support all those working for their relief.

And increase in us all a single-mindedness in your love; that all our wanderings of body, mind and spirit are finally gathered up into the homecoming of your Heaven. Through Christ our Lord. Amen.

Fifth Day • MORNING

I hear the singing of the summer grass.
And love, I find, has no considered end,

Nor is it subject to the wilderness
Which follows death. I am not traitor to
A person or a memory. I trace

Behind that love another which is running
Around, ahead. I need not ask its meaning.[11]

'Love, I find, has no considered end' . . . And that is why, my dear Lord, I realize now that you can and do walk with me through that wilderness of loss and bereavement and pain and grief and bewilderment. Because behind my aching lost love another runs, the Love which gave me that human relationship in the first place.

So all I can do, my Lord, is sit quietly and wonder at that greater, deeper Love that is everywhere, behind, around, ahead: and trust it. Trust that my lost loved ones are safe with you somewhere, though I cannot see or feel how. Trust that severed loves may yet be joined again, that disconnections can be wonderfully, healingly, re-connected if we trust them to you.

So here and now I do that, Lord. I offer you my trust for those aching losses that have marked my life and fill me with grief when I reflect on them:

I offer you my trust for _____ who died and is with me no more.
I offer you my trust for _____ who abandoned their love for me and went away.
I offer you my trust for _____ whom I myself failed in love.

And I bring before you now, Lord, all those this day struggling with terrible human loss, so numbed that they cannot cry out to you for themselves. The children, Lord, left parentless through famine, Aids, war, earthquake and flood. Those left when the soldier does not return from war. Those grieving over husbands, wives, children torn from them by civil strife and battles for land rights. O Father God, whose heart is large enough for the vast sum of our grief, hear us and send your strength and comfort and merciful justice to meet such needs.

For, Lord of Love, you know the cost of all loving and have paid the price in full. Gather our sad ends of relationships, broken through death or betrayal or coldness, and breathe into them, somehow, somewhere, in the time and place of your grace, your healing Spirit. That things dislocate might be joined, that in wholeness we might rejoice together in your presence. For, Lord God, Love is your meaning – for all of us, everywhere and always. Lord God, diffidently and wistfully, I give you here my trust for it. Amen.

Fifth Day • EVENING

O God, my God!
I praise you now for your hand on all my life:

For my conception and safe birth;
for my nurturing through childhood;
for education and for leisure skills;
for tenderness and love in my family and beyond.

For my dreams of what my life might be;
for the civilization in which I live, and my civil rights
within it;
for such gifts of mind and person as I have, and some
opportunities to use them.

For the work I have been able to do, and your sustaining
in its heaviness and toil;
for your presence with me in unemployment, sustaining
me in its emptiness and rejection.

For the times when money has been short, and you have
met my needs;
for the times when my income has been high, and you
have taught me generosity and stewardship.

For love in relationships, and the wonder of mutual
commitment;
for the mysterious gift of marriage: the hopefulness
of home-making, the joys of physical intimacy,
the slow learning of self-sacrifice and the glory of
faithfulness.

For children, the wonder and joy of them, and all the
fears and hopes for them;

for the renewing gift of their love, and your comfort
  when that disappoints.

For the companionship of friends, its tenderness and
  depth; for comfort in desolate bereavement.

For the pleasures of health and energy, and the care of
  doctors and nurses when they fail.

For your beautiful world, with its creatures, and the
  challenge to conserve it and them;
for far cities and strange peoples and the richness in
  learning of them.

For all simple joys; all gentle thoughts; all music, books,
  films and art that feed the mind and nourish the soul.

For your Church, in its many forms; for all who truly
  worship the one true God;
for the experience of the love of Christ in my life; for
  the joy of all who know him;
for the experience of eternal things in this life, and the
  hope of Heaven hereafter.

O God, my God, how shall I thank you? With all my
heart? Yes, Lord! Amen.

Sixth Day • MORNING

All earthly things that blessed morning
Were everlasting joy and warning . . .

O Christ who holds the open gate,
O Christ who drives the furrows straight,
O Christ the plough, O Christ the laughter
Of holy white birds flying after . . .

And we will walk the weeded field;
And tell the golden harvest's yield;
The corn that makes the holy bread
By which the soul of man is fed.
The holy bread, the food impressed,
Thy everlasting mercy, Christ.[12]

O Christ who holds the open gate, bring us through it. My people, Lord, my nation and my city, small town, village, housing estate . . . the people in this place where I live. Bring us, bring us through your open gate. Open our eyes to the 'everlasting joy and warning' in all earthly things around us. For you have messages for me wherever I look – that open gate can be into a factory or an office, you are not confined to rural idyll, my Lord, in your signals to us. Wherever I look, in trim suburb or high hill-top or battered high-rise or your lovely, lovely valleys of natural fruitfulness, there is a message, and it is about that everlasting mercy that spins the Earth and holds the universe in frame and reaches deep into our very souls to bring us home to you. O Lord, bring my people home to harvest, and I with them.

An 'everlasting joy and warning' – it's no easy, sentimental, facile message you have for me this day, Lord, is it? It never was.

The things of joy, all the experiences, small and great, which add up to a gladness at the heart of things – from my child's birth to an unexpected greeting in the morning's mail, to the one I most love and long for turning and saying, 'I love you', to sudden sunshine across the street – all these are also warnings. They say, *'There is joy for you and for all Creation, because there is mercy. And there is mercy because there needs to be mercy.'*

In my joy in your presence today in all things, dear Lord, let me not hide from myself all those things that question it: the sickness in our human societies, the seemingly casual cruelty of natural disasters, those things in myself of which I am ashamed that block my openness to you . . . Help me to face, clear-eyed and truthfully – as you did, my Lord, while among us – the things in us that work for our doom. And when I do so, Lord, then instead of being overwhelmed by them or turned away from you, help me to offer them to your profound and everlasting mercy. See, here I now name and offer my angers and doubts and uncertainties and fears for my world and my loved ones and myself: _____

Lord, I know that their power to destroy can be extinguished, in my life and in all Creation, by the holy energy of your profound and dynamic mercy. So I see the white birds flying and I eat your bread from the springing corn and I thank you, my Lord, for your daily and eternal joyous mercy in my life. O Lord, bring others to that joy. And may I always share it. Amen.

Sixth Day • EVENING

I am not moved to love thee, my Lord God
by heaven thou hast promised me;
I am not moved by the sore dreaded hell
to forbear me from offending thee.

I am moved by thee, Lord: I am moved
at seeing thee nailed upon the cross and mocked:
I am moved by thy body all over wounds:
I am moved by thy dishonour and thy death.

I am moved, last, by thy love, in such a wise
that though there were no heaven I still should love thee
and though there were no hell I still should fear thee.

I need no gift of thee to make me love thee,
for though my present hope were all despair,
as now I love thee I should love thee still.[13]

O Lord, I too am 'moved by thee' . . .
Let me in silence gaze at you.
Really gaze, Lord, not just glance.

. . .

Tonight I grieve over your wounds, and wonder at your
    love.
And, marvelling, offer you my future. And my heart.
Amen.

Seventh Day • MORNING

It is reported of the peacock that, priding himself in his
gay feathers, he ruffles them up, but spying his black feet,
he soon lets fall his plumes; so he that glories in his gifts
and adorning should look upon his corruptions, and that
will damp his high thoughts.[14]

Lord, I have black feet. I caught sight of them last night when I
was reviewing the day. And now as I face the morning I need to
look at them truthfully: now at this moment when they are not
hidden from me by other people's golden opinions (*there's* bright
plumage indeed, and most of it borrowed feathers). Not hidden
from me either by a false peacock glory of my own complacency.

For – here's the truth of it, Lord – such lovely adornings, such
gifts of person and mind and spirit, as I have, were none of my
achieving, but given, given, given by you, and brightest when
I display them not in peacock pride but as a glory that is yours.
So here and now I thank you for all that you have given me,
and I lay it before you again.

Lord, forgive me for the times I have taken sole credit for my
plumage (even privately, to myself). Keep me properly thankful for what I have been given. Yet help me not to diminish your
great generosity to me by some spurious humility, denying
your gifts' existence in me. Instead keep me full of wonder at
the plumage given.

And about those black feet. Help me not to hide them from
myself – or you. I lay before you now, alongside those bright
gift feathers you have given me, all the things about myself
I am ashamed of:

This _____
and this _____

28

Dear Lord, if I did not know that you forgive unconditionally and all the time, what darkness of spirit I would know now. But I know, with wonder, that you love me, all of me, even my black feet, and look very tenderly on my fear of others seeing them. And so I can let *you* see them without fear of losing your love and your gifts to me.

Lord, I pray now for those I know who are so frightened that if they don't keep their plumage ruffled out, their black feet will be visible and they will lose all value in others' eyes, and most of all in yours. Help us all to understand that you know all about our black feet and have no desire to 'dampen our high thoughts', but only to bring them fluttering home where they belong, with you.

So with such a heart I bring my own black feet, and those of my family and friends, to you, Lord. Forgive us, and keep us humbly aware of how utterly we depend on your grace to redeem, and your loving-kindness to clothe us in your bright feathers.

And renew in me the joy of displaying the plumage you have given me for *your* glory and *your* praise. Amen.

Seventh Day • EVENING

> The more I think of faith, more rare and good
> It seems, and even greater may it be
> Since all the world depends on it for peace.[15]

Yes, it is rare, Lord: it's rarer than it ought to be in my own life. Because though I know you as the God I can trust with my all, and I affirm that in public in worship and repeat it in private in my prayers, yet a lot of the time I don't live that way. Was that the way I lived today, Lord? Looking back, did faith shape today's living? . . .

I'm often afraid, Lord; or perplexed; or caught in difficult relationships. And somehow thoughtlessness or perhaps even pride ('I can deal with this') stops me bringing it immediately to you. And yet, like all the world, I depend on that faith, that trusting that you are in this situation, for my peace.

So keep me more constantly mindful, Lord, that it is your world, and I can trust you with it, all of it, even the harsh and terrible bits of it. That you are Lord of my patch, and all within it and from beyond it that affects my life.

And, O Lord, I long that others too should know how totally we can depend on you for our peace. Peace 'not as the world gives'; peace that is an inner core, a quietude, which holds us steady even though the Universe rocks. I know it, Lord. Help me live it enough to share it. For your love's sake. Amen.

Eighth Day • MORNING

A Chinese woman's prayer
after learning to read

We are going home to many who cannot read.
So, Lord, make us to be Bibles,
so that those who cannot read the Book
can read it in us.[16]

Lord, the truth is there are many in my own nation who can't 'read the Book': wholly ignorant of it, disconnected from it, even alienated from it. So, like this Chinese woman, I've got a responsibility. For I have the huge privilege of having learned to read your Word, and you have engaged me with it profoundly.

So if here in the UK I am among millions to whom your Word is closed, then it's up to me and others like me to be its living story today, its account in action in this time and this place; to be a Biblical way of being . . .

Lord, you know how fallible and feeble I am; how far from the power and dynamic and purity of your Word as it runs. But I can try; with your help I can try. Help me to reflect in my own life something of the wonder and grace that is available in your Word. And bless all those who search for meaning in life, and a God in whom they can trust, who have not yet found you. Draw them to you, and insofar as I can, let me shine a light on those pages, opaque to so many. For they are your lively oracles, my Lord, and offer hope to the dying. Thank you for them. Amen.

Eighth Day • EVENING

> O God, the problem with my anger unleashed
> is the same as that of my love tied up.
> It puts me at the centre
> and is the greatest idolatry.[17]

O my Lord, I cannot rest tonight because of my anger. And yet, Lord, I do not know how to be angry without sinning. Teach me, when:

— I am angry with those who have the means and the authority to alleviate poverty and homelessness, and do not do it.

— I am angry with those in your church who seem to care more for observances than the proclamation and living out of your astounding love.

— I am angry with politicians who spend their skill in clever political manipulation instead of risking their position to resolve hard issues.

— I am angry with those who lay waste the Earth's resources to line their own pockets, or who manipulate global markets regardless of consequence to creatures and humans alike.

— I am angry with bureaucrats careless of the anguish of asylum-seekers; I am angry with myself and my nation for being so rejecting of those seeking refuge.

— I am angry with those I live among, who do not carry their share of the load, or seem not to value me.

— Sometimes, Lord, I am even angry about the weather! (and not just the hurricanes).

O my Lord, I discern in my anger a sense of self-righteousness that is much too close to pleasure. And I think of you, Lord. You were never angry in your own defence, and you took no pleasure in anger: else why the Cross? But you were angry for God: you were angry with those who sold him as a commodity; you were angry with those who used him for their own status; or who treated him as belonging only to them.

O Lord, implant in me a holy fear of the wrong kind of anger, which ministers to my own sense of self-importance or is simply an indulgence of my own frustration. Forgive me, Lord, for all such occasions. I think particularly of _____ and _____

O Lord, keep me in awe of your holy anger, and let me never seek to counterfeit it. Forgive me, Lord, for all such occasions. I think particularly of _____ and _____

And let me live so close to you that should that rare moment come when I must speak out with your anger against the unholy, I may do so with conviction, selflessness and power. To the glory of God the Father. Amen.

Ninth Day • MORNING

May time, loveliest season,
Loud bird parley, new growth green,
Ploughs in furrow, oxen yoked,
Emerald sea, land-hues dappled.

When cuckoos call from fair tree-tops . . .

On hill, in vale, in ocean's isles,
Whichever way man goes,
Blest Christ there's no evading.[18]

Eight centuries later, and how instantly recognizable is the loveliness of a May morning in this thirteenth-century Welsh song. How instantly recognizable, too, Lord, the surge of joy with which we respond not just to the beauty of springtime with its renewal of life and freshness all around, but to the Lord of life of whom it speaks. On hill, in vale, in ocean's isles, whichever way we go, there's no evading our blest Lord Jesus in this breaking forth of joyous new life.

Whichever way we go – and so, Lord, that's true in the towns and cities as well as in your fair countryside. So teach me to look for you as the Lord of resurgent life in this month of May in urban landscape.

Lord, you are here in the calling and fluttering of your birds in the shrubs behind my neighbour's house.

You are here in the sunlight slanting between the tall houses and cobbling the ginnels with light.

You are here in the light flashing across a thousand car windows passing along the road bridge in the distance.

You are here in the stocky figure playing his Northumbrian pipes on the road from the bus station to the town.

You are here in the sunlit striped awnings above the market stalls, and in the plenitude and variety of what the farmers' market is offering.

You are here in the cheerful greetings we give each other as we hurry along, sharing our pleasure in the beauty of the day.

You are here in the children dancing in their new sandals; you are here in the cat sunning its warm fur on the top of the wall; you are here in the ducklings bobbing in flotilla behind their quacking parent.

You are here in the bright anoraks and light rucksacks of the hikers setting off for the station; here in the light streaming through the stained-glass windows as I stop to salute you in the city centre church.

You are here, Lord, here in the bright dust of the ground and the hazy blue sky above us; here in the rising clamour of the streets as the noonday crowd thickens; here within me and around me and above and below me, in all I see and all I know.

O Lord, you are Life and you are everywhere, and I praise you for your goodness. Keep me mindful of all this, dear Lord, when the summer rains come and the sky darkens: that I may know you there too, and rejoice in your pattern of summer and winter, seedtime and harvest, working out your purposes for our earth, and promised as long as Earth – and we – remain. Amen.

Ninth Day • EVENING

That night I awoke lying upon my back and hearing a voice speaking about me and saying: 'No human soul is like any other human soul, and therefore the love of God for any human soul is infinite, for no other human soul can satisfy the same need in God.'[19]

Lord, when I thank you, in the words of the General Thanksgiving, for my 'creation, preservation, and all the blessings of this life', I don't usually stop to explore with wonder the mystery and miracle of your creation of *me*. Of me as a unique creation, Lord, fashioned by you in the midst of millions through time, and yet wholly individual. Thank you for this reminder of what is unique about me, Lord. Not my physique or my colouring, such gifts and defects of mind, body and spirit as are mine. Nothing of that is necessarily unique, and I may be 'the image' of my twin, or bear a strong family likeness, and know all too well the disposition of my inherited genes. But still I am unique, Father, for you want me to be me, uniquely me, in the response I, and only I, can give to your love.

O my Lord God, it is a debt I owe and only I can pay. So draw out from me, my Lord, the response only I can give. Help me remember this in those times when I find it difficult to say the words of that thanksgiving, for my own creation and preservation, when I have so low a notion of myself and my own acceptability to people – and to you? – that the words won't come from the heart. Help me, and those like me who suffer such loss of self-esteem, to turn to you and be caught up in the glory, the infinite breadth and depth, of the Love that is incomplete unless I put *my* hand out into the strong clasp of the living God. So again, now, Lord, I put my hand into yours. Keep it there. Amen.

Tenth Day • MORNING

The prayer of the little bird

Dear God,
I don't know how to pray by myself
very well,
but will You please
protect my little nest from wind and rain?
Put a great deal of dew on the flowers,
many seeds in my way.
Make Your blue very high,
Your branches lissom,
let Your kind light stay late in the sky
and set my heart burning with such music
that I must sing, sing, sing . . .
Please, Lord.[20]

Any one of the tumble of small birds in my bushes and swinging from the feeders above my patio could be praying this right now. So I will join them. For, dear Lord, we are all your little birds and you look on us with that same love that spoke of the sparrows sold for two farthings, known to and cared about by the Father God. And you taught us, like this little bird, to pray for our daily needs – shelter and food and drink – because our Father knows we have need of such things.

So I bring to you here my prayer as one of your little birds. Keep my home safe, dear Lord, for myself and all who share it. (And now as I pray that prayer I see the shelterless and unhoustelled of the earth, Father . . . O Lord, teach me how to have a sheltering heart for all such.)

Keep my home safe from all that would threaten it: the wind and rain of material disaster, and, more destructive, from tempests of strife within the home. And help me put food on the table for all who need it – make my table wide enough.

And give me and my loved ones, my Lord, space for our souls and minds and bodies to explore and grow in your great blue sky of infinite knowledge and understanding, leading us into wider and deeper and higher ways of being. And make the branches of our skills ever more lissom, that we may make, and do, beautifully for you and for the world.

And nightfall comes to our lives by your gift, dear Lord. If it is right for me, let your kind light stay long in my life's sky, and in those most dear to me. Here I name them _____

But most of all, whether my days be long or short, fill my heart to the brim daily with praise. To you, my Lord: let me sing, sing, sing. Amen.

Tenth Day • EVENING

King Jesus hath a garden full of divers flowers
Where I go culling posies gay, all times and hours,
There naught is heard but the Paradise bird, harp,
   dulcimer and lute,
With cymbal, trump and tymbal,
And the tender soothing flute.

Ah! Jesu Lord, my heart and weal, my bliss complete,
Make thou my heart thy garden-plot, fair trim and neat.
That I may hear this music clear, the Paradise bird,
With cymbal, trump and tymbal
And the tender soothing flute.[21]

Truth is, your garden is everywhere I go, my King Jesus: unexpected corners of it wherever I turn. So tonight I look back down the day and dwell in thankfulness on my glimpses of your garden in it:

As I walked down that grimy city street, as I travelled down that featureless suburban development, as I sat in that traffic jam, as I stood in that queue; suddenly, blooming there before me in the life of the street and in the rooms I entered, were bright clusters of your flowers. Blossoms of small kindnesses, swelling buds of friendships, tassels of gentleness, tall white lilies of truthfulness, deep red roses of courage, and everywhere the strong green shoots of hope. Only, Lord, today, as so often, I was at risk of being too preoccupied with my own affairs, and so nearly missed the bright delight there before me, let alone gathered these posies to offer to others or to make more beautiful a room in my life. So now I call them to mind, every hint and glimpse of them _____

Open my eyes this night to the garden you gave me today,
King Jesus.

So may I hear the music that chimes in it, gentle, constant. The joyous singing of the Paradise bird – O lovely, brilliant, living creature! – and behind him, sounding softly but very clearly, all the musical instruments of Heaven. Lord, I walk daily among such music. But so often, immersed in myself, I don't hear it.

Open my ears this night to the music you gave me today,
King Jesus.

For when, my Lord Gardener, I begin to notice your flowers everywhere, I find that some seeds have blown from them into my own heart, and have taken root, and blossomed. And then, very faintly, I hear the music sounding softly in my own heart too; and as he sings, I glimpse – O lovely flash of rainbow colour – the Paradise bird.

Tend my heart tonight as one of your small gardens,
my dear King Jesus.
Make it beautiful for your delight.
May it give a little joy to others.
May its diffident music utter, in its own small notes,
The joy of your praise.
Amen.

Eleventh Day • MORNING

What no person has a right to, is to delude others into the belief that faith is something of no great significance, or that it is an easy matter, whereas it is the greatest, and most difficult, of all things.[22]

The only thing that counts is faith working through love.
(*Galatians 5.6*)

There's this little carving on my wall, Lord, in black oak, brought from Canterbury Cathedral. He's a fully armed knight, creeping with drawn sword towards his victim, that priest at your altar, an archbishop who had confronted a king.

Faith was the greatest thing of all for that priest, Lord, expressing itself in love for his people, his church. He would die for it. But it was faith – another sort of faith – that took that creeping knight and his fellows to Canterbury to do murder. And it was faith – another sort of faith – that motivated their king in his death-wish for his archbishop.

So, Lord, I need to look at my faiths. What faiths do I have? How do they show themselves? What am I prepared to act for? Live for? Die for?

I have faith in my family and friends, Lord. I trust them, act for them, lay myself out for them, because I love them.

Lord, keep me in that faith even if they let me down.
(For that's the faith you keep with us, Lord.)
Lord, keep them in that faith when I let them down . . .

I have faith in the way of life you have called me to. The task you have given me. Even when the going is rough and I don't seem to be achieving anything, I strive for it, act in it, lay myself out for it; because that is love for you expressing itself in action . . .

Lord, keep me in that faith even when I seem to be in a cul-de-sac.
Lord, keep me in that faith even when I'm a failure.

I have faith in your Church, Lord, your people of God, and so I strive for her, act for her, lay myself out for her.

Lord, keep me in that faith even when I'm ashamed of what the Church is doing and being.
Lord, keep me in that faith when I myself fall short of what the Church asks.

But, Lord God, none of these faiths would make any sense if they didn't grow out of, weren't kept in perspective by, my faith in you. If all my trusting, striving, acting, caring, isn't rooted in *your* trusting, striving, acting, caring . . . then they won't amount to much.

Lord, I believe.
Help me to express that faith daily in love.
Starting – again – with today.
Amen.

Eleventh Day • EVENING

Prayer of the tortoise

I am coming,
One must take nature as she is!
It was not I who made her!
I do not mean to criticize
this house on my back –
It has its points –
but you must admit, Lord,
it is heavy to carry!
Still,
let us hope that this double enclosure,
my shell and my heart,
will never be quite shut to you.[23]

Snails obey the will of God . . . slowly.[24]

Yes, I *am* coming, Lord, but like the tortoise and the snail my following after you is very, very slow . . . Because that seems to be the way I am, Lord; and I see as you look at me that you know and accept that this is the best I can manage. That I am coming to you in my own slow, cautious way, quite different from the lively, eager, dancing response of many of your other creatures. Help me not to envy them, Lord, but to obey you in the way you made me, which is the only offering you expect, or even want, from such as me. Like the tortoise and the snail I am one of those made to carry my house on my back: all the things I need to keep me safe and secure and functioning in my own small way in the world for you.

It means, Lord, that I don't travel light, as some do. But you gave them to me, Lord, so here I thank you for them and lay them before you for your blessing:

my home _____
my family _____
my friends _____
my work and interests _____
my health _____
my beautiful world _____
all that is life-giving and sustaining in my existence
_____
all those difficulties of life you help me overcome _____
all those whose often unseen kindness has made
my life better _____

Lord, you have wrapped me in the protections I need. Help me, while accepting them gratefully, never, never, never, dear Lord, to let them close me off from you. Amen.

Twelfth Day • MORNING

> Put peace into each other's hands
> and like a treasure hold it,
> protect it like a candle flame,
> with tenderness enfold it.
>
> Put peace into each other's hands
> with loving expectation;
> be gentle in your words and ways
> in touch with God's creation . . .
>
> Put Christ into each other's hands,
> he is love's deepest measure;
> in love make peace, give peace a chance,
> and share it like a treasure.[25]

So this is what we do when we gather together in worship round your holy table, Lord. Putting peace in each other's hands is simple and natural, then.

But what about today, Lord? As I go out to face my daily situations, how do I put peace into others' hands there? In our Christian gathering we are receptive, we look to receive from each other, through each other, the gift of your peace. But out there where I must do my living today, very few people will be holding out a hand in peace. There are more curled fists than cupped hands out there.

And yet it is an imperative of your life in us that we find a way. So today, Lord:

Help me protect and treasure all that makes for peace in my thoughts of others, and my conversations with them.

Help me, where I find myself in a situation where there is violence of word or intention, to be brave enough to refuse it and instead engage it with your peace.

Help me respond with gentleness even when others are treating me roughly by word or action; even when others are misrepresenting me, or treating me with sarcastic contempt or angry attack.

(How do I do that, Lord? Only if I hold on to you doing it for me, as you did in Galilee and Jerusalem . . .)

Help me notice, today, when someone else is struggling to be 'gentle in their words and ways', and honour and support them in it.

O Lord Jesus, peace is so rare and fragile and precious a plant, and yet our ultimate well-being grows from it. It is your gift to us and we lose sight of it so quickly, caught up in the satisfactions of righteous indignation about this or that cause. Help me, help me to play my own small part in tending that precious root of peace, that it may spread and multiply in this bit of your kingdom. To your honour, Lord. Amen.

For when the night is very dark

My harvest withers. Health, my means to live –
All things seem rushing straight into the dark –
But the dark still is God . . .
The hairs I made not, thou art numbering.
Thou art my life – I the brook, thou the spring.
Because thine eyes are open, I can see;
Because thou art thyself, there I am me.[26]

'The dark still is God . . .' O Lord God, can that be true even of *this* darkness? Do you rule here, where everything that matters seems to have gone, where the pain is too great and I cry out for release? Where I seem to be slowly bleeding away within; and worse, where I have to watch one I love suffering so? O help me, help me, Lord, to be willing to know you here and so be less afraid. Help me not to beat my spirit against this darkness with nostalgia or bitterness, but look deep within for some sign of your presence. *Because thine eyes are open, can I see?* Are you at work, Lord, even here, even now?

And if I can't, Lord, simply can't, make any move towards you, even with a glance, then let me at least hold on to the certainty that you know and understand. Because you have been there. Because you have been there. Bring me through, O my Lord God, bring me through. Amen. Amen.

Thirteenth Day • MORNING

> God's work of art.
> That's me?
> Then beauty must lie
> In the eye of the
> Beholder.

Lord, I don't take seriously enough your creative delight in me. It's so difficult to think of myself as a 'unique work of art' into which you pour your energy for pure joy of making. Help me grasp again the wonder of it: that you are my Creating God. For you are shaping me throughout my life to become, become, become – what? That which your eye, and yours only, discerns I might be, if I let you love me, with however severe a love, into the full glory of which each of us under your shaping hand is capable. So:

> Go on, Lord.
> Love me into wholeness.
> Set me free
> To share with you
> In your creative joy;
> To laugh with you
> At your delight
> In me
> Your work of art.[27]

For when I get to that point, Lord, then I share with you too your creative joy in all your other works of art. And I long that all your Creation, the good Earth and all that it inhabit, the universes beyond universes and the mystery of all the dark materials still inconceivably beyond our measuring – I long that all should be freed into your purpose as your vast and wonderful work of art, shaped into the ultimate wholeness that is, beyond our imagining, your design.

So today, Lord, I pray, enact in this world by your hidden power whatever will free us into what you want us to be. So that all Creation declares your glory; and so that I play my small part in the dynamic of your creating. Amen.

Thirteenth Day • EVENING

Lord God, thank you for the prayers handed down to us by your faithful men and women of the past. Help me to learn from them the marvels of love and faithfulness and generosity and holiness that ordinary folk have shown when their total trust is in you. O Lord, nurture my spirit, by whatever means are necessary, to the kind of Christ-like understanding of your love, and living by it, which inspired this prayer amid the horrors of Ravensbruck:

> O Lord, remember not only the men and women of good will, but also those of ill will. But do not remember all the suffering they have inflicted on us; remember the fruits we have bought, thanks to this suffering – our comradeship, our loyalty, our humility, our courage, our generosity, the greatness of heart which has grown out of all this; and when they come to judgment let all the fruits which we have borne be their forgiveness.[28]

O Lord, when I fear for myself or my loved ones the threat of others' violence or greed, or fanatical desire for power, bring to my mind those who have suffered the darkest horrors at the hands of others, and have conquered, in your power, both fear and bitterness.

O Lord, when I react to slights and minor injuries as though they were deadly and unassuageable wounds, bring to my mind those who have suffered the most terrible wounds at the hands of others, and have conquered, in your power, both fear and bitterness.

O Lord, when in anger I cannot pray for those who have acted or spoken to me as though they were enemies to me, bring to my mind those who have suffered the most savage hostility at the hands of others, and have conquered, in your power, both fear and bitterness.

O Lord, help me look away from myself and my fears and resentments to the wonder of what you can do with human lives, and the fruits you can nurture in them even in vile places. So may I not so much lament the wickedness of which we are capable as marvel at the goodness you can create in us. May it be so in my life, Lord. Amen.

Fourteenth Day • MORNING

Let us reach beyond the things we cannot understand to
the God we trust.

(A tombstone at Knebworth)

The news from the Holy Land, the place you graced for ever
with your physical presence, is so terrible, my Lord Christ. Peoples
locked in combat over sacred soil, in hatred committing unthink-
able outrages against each other. Babies torn apart by suicide
bombers in the shopping streets. Whole rows of dwellings
bulldozed while their dazed occupants look on, their broken
belongings trampled in the dust. And the holy men of each
side claiming the anger of the Most Holy God against the
enemy. And through it all that appalling concrete wall marches
through communities and lives, disrupting everything in its
way, hideous and merciless and opaque to any kind of reason
or compromise.

Such walls march through our human history, Lord God, and
how they must grieve your heart. The Berlin Wall, a symbol of
the worst kind of repression, and its fall a magnificent image
of the human spirit breaking through its political chains at last.
The walls in Northern Ireland, Lord; and back, back, right
through history beyond even Hadrian's Wall to the Great Wall
of China.

Lord, when I look back at our human history, and when
I look round now at the ferocity of conflict in so many places
this very day, I do not understand how you could want to have
anything to do with us, far less love us enough to bear on
our behalf what we do to each other. Sometimes I want you to
intervene like cavalry coming over the hill, and like so many in
despair and anguish I cry out, 'How long, O Lord? How long?'

And then I look at the Cross and see the only sort of God one can trust: the God among us. Not aiming a heavenly missile from some divine height, but sadly gathering together for the dispossessed what survives of their belongings, and then picking up the crying children and carrying them to whatever rough shelter is available. Not a God of heroic incident, but the God who is here all the time with us, slowly rebuilding broken homes and broken lives:

> To say God intervenes
> Suggests occasional acts –
> Throughout our universe
> The Giver interacts.[29]

You interact with us all the time, Lord: all the time you are there. So we must look for you in every murderous incident and every confrontation of peoples whose bloodstained history will always give them just cause, if they seek it, for further outrage. *For you are there, always there, in the pity of it, the pity of it.*

Teach me how to build on that pity, Lord. Teach me how to grieve in the right way, and then give all I can, by word and act and prayer and gift, to move peace just a little nearer, to dissolve ancient hatreds by just that one small inch, to dispel prejudice and open understanding just a fraction nearer truth. And keep me patient and open-hearted when I am tempted not to be.

And I pray for the peace of Jerusalem. May her terrible wall fall, one day, not needed any more . . . And be replaced with the jasper walls of your promised Holy City, O Lord. Amen.

Fourteenth Day • EVENING

Christ who knows all his sheep
Will all in safety keep;
He will not lose his blood
Nor intercession,
Nor we the purchased good
Of his dear passion.

I know my God is just
To him I wholly trust
All that I have and am
All that I hope for.
All's sure and seen to him
Which here I grope for.

Lord Jesus, take my spirit,
I trust thy love and merit,
Take home this wandering sheep
For thou hast sought it;
This soul in safety keep
For thou hast bought it.[30]

'All's sure and seen to him/Which here I grope for.' O Lord God, I am so grateful to lean back against the certainty of your complete understanding. I grope about, trying to find my right way forward in what often feels like the dark: not in great moral dilemmas, most of the time, Lord, but in those multitudinous small decisions that make the texture of our days, and in the end add up to a life of obedience or of self-will. And so often my intentions are good, Lord, yearning to be your faithful child. But I misjudge or misread the issues, or matters turn out quite differently from my expectations, and somehow I've got into the bogs of waywardness without knowing quite how.

So to know you *know*, Father, and have seen not just the outcome but the struggle, is deep comfort. You know where my feet are on the path at this minute, and how boggy it all feels, and how hard the hill ahead looks. And you also know just where that path is winding to, up there among those distant hills; and what view will break on my wondering eyes when I reach the path's end.

And most comforting of all is your promise that you will get me there, that through my Lord Jesus Christ you will get me there. I thank you, I thank you that you have called me wholly to trust in you and in your dealings with me, however mysterious and even hurtful they might seem. I look back over the journey so far and marvel:

at precipices narrowly avoided; I remember _____
at cold hard hills surmounted; I remember _____
at sweet pastures rested in; I remember _____
at your sheltering in bitter winter storms; I remember

_____

at times of being woefully lost and crying out to you, and lo, you were there, picking me up and laying my bruised being on your shoulder and carrying me out of danger; I remember _____

O Lord Christ, how good and great a shepherd you have been to me. So I pray now for your other wanderers. Lord God, gather them in; gather them in, where they are lost or stuck in a morass or trembling on a high precipice, or even wandering happily unaware of the dangers or how far they are from home. O Lord my Shepherd, I pray for your other sheep – whom you have sought –

all our souls in safety keep
which you have bought.
Amen.

Fifteenth Day • MORNING

Waiting for the echo . . .

Publishing a volume of verse is like dropping a rose petal down the Grand Canyon and waiting for an echo . . .[31]

The truth is, Lord, that's often what it feels like when I'm praying. And sometimes it feels as though I'm running out of rose petals, and sometimes I'm just weary, weary of waiting for the echo.

Why should talking to you feel so one-sided a lot of the time, Lord? We come to you daily, and sometimes there you are, welcoming and warm and shining in our hearts, and we enjoy easy dialogue as with an intimate friend. And we know there is no place – *no* place – where we would rather be than here in your presence in loving exchange of understanding. Our rose petals then are multitudinous and brilliant in colour, like coloured snowflakes which though so minute and fragile can in their accumulation stop trains and bury mountains. And we wonder why we ever found talking to you difficult.

And then, with no warning, we can feel and hear you no longer. *Deus absconditus* . . . you are gone. Then, oh then, prayer has to become much, much more than easy converse with you. I find, if I stay faithful in my seeking, that praying then becomes the radio signal sent out into the lonely ether, the voice-mail as yet apparently uncollected, the ship's horn sounding its melancholy note in the fog, the winking light through empty darkness, simple notes of music echoing in the dead emptiness of a cave; it becomes our Morse code, our tapping on the walls of our prison cell in the hope of response.

O Lord Christ, when ordinary talking with you seems no longer possible, teach me, teach me that other ways of communicating with you are as valid, and as precious to you. So keep me sending out the voice-mail, tapping out the Morse code and listening for your response, in whatever form you choose to make it. For your answer comes, always – eventually; it comes, though long-delayed and rarely in the form expected.

And, Lord Jesus, I thank you that this universal human experience of the absent God, the forsaking God, you have yourself redeemed and blessed by suffering it in your own anguished soul. When the blankness of Heaven becomes too great for me, so that, almost, I cannot sustain it, let me lose myself in your desolate cry: 'My God! My God! Why have you forsaken me?' And so keep me faithful not through my own will but through your blessing; that one day I may find myself caught up in that sweet conversation that is the dialogue of Heaven itself.

Lord God, I believe.
In times of blankness, help my unbelief.
Through Jesus Christ our Lord.
Amen.

Fifteenth Day • EVENING

And all the wickedness in this world –
  that men might work or think,
Is no more to the mercy of God –
  than a live coal in the sea.[32]

Lord, I can't sleep tonight for sickness of heart at the evil I've been hearing about on the news. There is, of course, the never-ending tale of terrorist acts and brutal civil disorders all across the world. But this is more particularized and much, much more local. A three-month-old baby, Lord, a few miles from here, battered to death by a violently jealous father after, it now becomes clear, having been tortured all its terrible little life. *And you let it happen, Lord.* You let it happen. You didn't intervene . . .

Of course, it is we too who let it happen, and again there is the sorry tale of failed care services. And they act on behalf of me, and my nation: and if they fail, I carry some of the responsibility, for it is my civic responsibility to press for proper care whatever the cost. But while we wrangle politically about responsibility, that little scrap has endured ninety-odd days of agony. O Lord, where were you? Where were you? . . .

And then I look at the Cross and I know where you were. Right there in that baby's suffering, battered in innocence as you have been by us for 2,000 years. The crucified one; always the crucified one.

And that's when I can't get my head round the huge mystery of your mercy on our evil, Lord. Because you endure it all not just for the minor petty sinners like me, but your mercy is so huge that it contains and extinguishes the unimaginable evil of that baby-torturing father. And all sadistic and hating figures who creep out of our human nightmare. William Langland, who lived through the horrors of the Black Death and the terrible uncertainties of his century, had so strong a grasp on the kind of God you are that he could give us the marvellously vivid picture above: your mercy extinguishing all the evil we can do or even imagine as simply as one live coal in the vast seas.

Lord, when my faith is shaken by the sudden immediacy of a local example of our wickedness, let me not refuse the horror and grief of the suffering involved. But help me hold on to you while I grieve over *us* and what we are. Because instead of walking away from us, my Lord, you walked towards us and put yourself in that baby's place. For all time. I do not know how, in some unimaginable way, your mercy helped that baby. But I do believe it is large enough one day to quench the wickedness that killed that baby. And so I must trust it, and learn from it.

And so, tonight, Lord, I pray for two people. I pray for that small scrap of humanity that he may at this very moment know the full wonder of your radiant and healing love in the glory of Heaven. And I pray for that wicked and impenitent father that you may break through to him with your terrible mercy and bring him to a place where he can no longer avert his eyes from your just and loving gaze.

And I ask, Lord God, that this night you have mercy on all those tempted to terrible evil. And I ask, Lord God, that you forgive me my sins of this day, including any complicity I have had, through complacency or lack of social will, in the suffering of neglected little ones. Through Jesus Christ who came to us as a vulnerable child. Amen.

Sixteenth Day • MORNING

Heaven shall not wait
for the poor to lose their patience,
the scorned to smile,
the despised to find a friend:
Jesus is Lord,
he has championed the unwanted;
in him injustice
confronts its timely end.

Heaven shall not wait
for the rich to share their fortunes,
the proud to fall,
the elite to tend the least:
Jesus is Lord;
he has shown the master's privilege –
to kneel and wash
servants' feet before they feast.

Heaven shall not wait
for the dawn of great ideas,
thoughts of compassion
divorced from cries of pain:
Jesus is Lord;
he has married word and action
his cross and company
make his purpose plain.[33]

I hate, I despise your festivals,
  and I take no delight in your solemn assemblies.
Even though you offer me your burnt-offerings and
  grain-offerings,

I will not accept them; . . .
Take away from me the noise of your songs;
    I will not listen to the melody of your harps.
But let justice roll down like waters,
    And righteousness like an ever-flowing stream.

(Amos 5.21–24)

Lord God, some of the worship we offer is beautiful, as exquisite as a carefully trained choir, a brilliant organist, a well-rehearsed reading, a carefully modulated sermon and finely crafted prayers can be. But tonight I am so shamed, as a member of your worshipping community, by these readings. For you speak across the centuries to your fervent worshippers and your message is unchanged: the only worship acceptable to you, beautiful in your eyes, my Lord God, is that which marries word and action in the name of Christ. How divorced are our lovely words of compassion from the cries of pain all around us in the streets? How truly do we share our fortunes? In what real sense have I washed anyone's feet today, that justice might be on the move and sheer goodness be honoured – no temporizing, no 'if only I could', but somewhere, somehow, have I championed the unwanted?

If I have not, Lord, forgive. Accept this prayer of contrition as the best I can give, and send me out in the power of your impatient Heaven to confront injustice, even to my own hurt. And keep me zealous that the holy beauty of the worship I bring you is always, always, by my deeds as well as words, making plain your purpose through truly sharing, publicly, both your company and your Cross. Amen.

Sixteenth day • EVENING

> Therefore is Love leader of the Lord's folk in heaven,
> And, to know its nature, it is nurtured in power,
> And in the heart is its home and fountainhead.
> Instinctively at heart a strength is stirring
> Flowing to the Father that formed us all,
> Looked on us with love, and let his Son die,
> Meekly, for our mis-doings, to amend us all.[34]

O Father God, who 'looked on us with love', as I gaze back over my years I am full of wonder at the way you have nurtured and protected me in all times of need. Of myself I can do so little, Lord God: if I start trying to do things my way, I wander and stumble and get it all dreadfully wrong. Forgive me for all the times, recent and long-buried, when I have done that.

But when I make the Lord Jesus Christ, your Son – your gift to us – welcome into what is the right home for your love-offering, my heart, then I am drawn into that lovely movement that flows directly to you, my Father God, and I am sustained and comforted and directed, instinct with the strength that is yours not mine. Thank you, Father God who formed us all, for the love that leads us from our earliest beginnings even to our right end, gathered into that glorious company who ever rejoice with you in Heaven:

> Love, the most pleasant thing our Lord pleads of us,
> Is also the ready roadway, running into Heaven.

Bring me into that ready roadway, my Lord. Amen.

Seventeenth Day • MORNING

The fairest thing we can experience is the mysterious . . .
He who knows it not and can no longer wonder, no
longer feel amazement, is as good as dead, a snuffed-out
candle. A knowledge of the existence of something we
cannot penetrate, of the manifestations of the profoundest
reason and the most radiant beauty . . . it is this
knowledge and this emotion that constitutes the truly
religious attitude.[35]

It's about 'wonder' as our proper dimension, isn't it, Lord?
Here identified by one of our greatest ever mathematicians,
Albert Einstein, as essential to our well-being. About living in
a condition of wonder, childlike wonder, at the extraordinary
mystery of the works of God as we see them around us and
within us, every day; and at the extraordinary mystery of God
himself.

And Heaven will be when that wonder is united at last with
knowledge of God, and understanding of his ways, while yet re-
maining 'wonder', the true element within which his Creation
thrives. Then the richness of all that mathematics, chemistry,
physics, astronomy, biological and botanical studies; all that
psychology and sociology and economics can show us becomes
suffused with glory, the glory of that profoundest and most radi-
antly beautiful reason, the mind and will of the Creator.

For even the little we know of beauty in these our finite lives
we find deeply mysterious, Lord. We pin the butterfly to trace
that mystery: but still we cannot by doing so probe or define
that beauty. When we climb the mountain and measure and map
it, still we have not expressed the mystery of its majesty. When
we search space and photograph and take samples from the far

planets, still we have not begun to define their extraordinary beauty and the power those images have to move our hearts.

So, Lord, bless all those who work to push out the boundaries of our knowledge; but keep us wondering. Bless our maps and our probes and our measurements; but keep us wondering. As one of our early great scientists, Francis Bacon, prayed:

> To God the Father, God the Word, God the Spirit . . . we humbly and earnestly beg, that Human things may not prejudice such as are Divine; neither that from unlocking of the gates of sense, and the kindling of a greater natural light, anything of incredulity or intellectual night may arise in our minds towards the Divine Mysteries. But rather that by our mind thoroughly cleansed and purged from fancy and vanities, and yet subject and perfectly given up to the Divine Oracles, there may be given unto Faith the things that are Faith's. Amen.[36]

. . . And to Holy Wonder the things that belong to Wonder. Amen.

Seventeenth Day • EVENING

Almighty Father, Son and Holy Ghost, eternal ever-blessed
gracious God; to me the least of saints, to me allow that I
may keep a door in Paradise. That I may keep even the
smallest door, the furthest, darkest, coldest door, the door
that is least used, the stiffest door. If so it be but in your
house, O God, if so it be that I can see your glory even
from afar, and hear your voice, O God, and know that
I am with you, O God. Amen.[37]

It's about what I really want from life, isn't it, Lord? What I
really most deeply and truly want, when the choices are absolute. And what I want is to belong to your people for ever, and
not to any of the alternatives.

You have given me glimpses of that kind of contentment
already, on a human scale, dear Lord. The deep security sometimes of hearing, from the room where I am working or resting,
the voices in other parts of the house of those I love, who share
this home permanently or temporarily. The sound of the children shouting in the garden, the clatter of activity from the
kitchen, even the teenage argument going on in the room below
. . . For such moments are (at their best!) about belonging in
an unquestioned, wholly accepted way within this little family
community, each of us with our proper and valued place and
role. And I thank you, thank you, thank you for them.

And I want to know that same sense of belonging with you
and your family, Father God. I want to belong with those who
love and serve the Lord Jesus. I want to belong to that company bonded together by the kind Holy Spirit, who guides our
way and teaches us how to express our truest longings.

I just want to be there, Lord God, in the house of Heaven where your rule is delighted in by all. Where to live is to obey spontaneously, with joy and without struggle. Where the over-flowing of our hearts in love is a perpetual song of happiness that we are, at last, entirely at home with the Father of goodness.

O my Father God, what role or position I might have in such a house or gathering is utterly unimportant. Indeed, Lord, it is the smallest niche, well out of the public eye, that would best fit who I am. Just one of those on the edge of the crowd, but able to serve in some small unnoticeable way that adds to the sum of Heaven's joy.

And because that is so, you teach me that Heaven reaches also into this life I live here and now. And so here and now I can delight in my belonging to your people and serving you, even though in small and unnoticed ways. And if I have wanted to fulfil some major service for you here, and you have gently but firmly directed me away from it, open my heart to the joy of whatever minor, unsung role you are asking: for that is sufficiency. So help me understand how my ordinary doings of today already have their place in the house of Heaven, and are fitting and training me for that service which will be unimaginably lovely and unimaginably for ever. And knowing that, and seeing my 'today' in the light of that, may I overflow with your happy praise in my actions and decisions, my think-ing and my speaking, and in all my loves and friendships. Through Christ who keeps me. Amen.

Eighteenth Day • MORNING

Rejoice in God, O ye Tongues!
Give the glory to the Lord, and the Lamb.
Nations and languages, and every
Creature in which is the breath of life.
Let man and beast appear before him
And magnify his name together . . .

For the flowers are great blessings
For the flowers are great blessings
For the flowers have their angels
   even the words of God's creation.
For the flower glorifies God
   and the root parries the adversary.
For there is a language of flowers,
For flowers are peculiarly the poetry of Christ . . .

Hallelujah from the heart of God
   and from the hand of the artist inimitable
   and from the echo of the heavenly harp
   A sweetness magnifical and mighty.

Hallelujah   Hallelujah   Hallelujah[38]

O gentle Lord, who fills your wounded ones with such an intensity of joy that they can speak your praise beyond all ordinary measure: thank you for this glorious song in praise of your Creation, from one whom his world defined as 'silly fellow', and treated as mad. Help me to join, now, at this moment, with all your creatures, human and beast, past and present, in passionate delight at the wonder of your glory both in this world and in that to come. Teach me to sing daily my small Amen to such psalms of thankfulness and full-hearted praise, nothing held back.

And out of that thankfulness for the wonder of Creation, Lord, may my actions and lifestyle grow: so that how I tend and care for the planet is also a psalm of praise. Teach me to shape a way of life that accords with the language of the flowers as the poetry of Christ, so that what I do to the Earth in my time upon it adds to its beauty and wonder rather than diminishing it. And accept, O Lord, my striving that my whole generation may thus seek Creation's good, as part of my song of delight at your *sweetness magnifical* . . . Amen.

Hallelujah. Hallelujah. Hallelujah.

Eighteenth Day • EVENING

Glory to Thee, my God this night
For all the blessings of the light;
Keep me, O keep me, King of Kings
Beneath thine own almightly wings.

Forgive me, Lord, for thy dear Son,
The ill that I this day have done,
That with the world, myself and thee
I ere I sleep at peace may be.

Teach me to live that I may dread
The grave as little as my bed;
Teach me to die, that so I may
Rise glorious at the aweful day.

O may my soul on thee repose,
And with sweet sleep my eyelids close,
Sleep that may me more vigorous make
To serve my God when I awake.

When in the night I sleepless lie,
My soul with heavenly thoughts supply;
Let no ill dreams disturb my rest,
No powers of darkness me molest.[39]

Let it be so, Lord, for your name's sake; trusting in which, I will
lay me down in peace and take my rest; for it is thou, Lord,
only, that makest me dwell in safety.

Nineteenth Day • MORNING

Now another day is breaking,
Sleep is sweet and so is waking.
Dear Lord, I promised you last night
Never again to sulk or fight.
Such vows are easier to keep
When a child is sound asleep.
Today, O Lord, for your dear sake,
I'll try and keep them when awake.[40]

'Dear Lord, I promised you last night' . . .

Thank you for what I understood last night, Lord, of the day's journey and where it had taken me in my heart. Let me look again, freshly this morning, at yesterday's travel: and ask for your forgiveness on any wrong turnings and lost opportunities; and thank you for all that was good in it, bringing me safely to today.

So take yesterday, Lord, and do in my heart what is needed for it.

I thank you, my Lord.

And then there was the night's rest. Thank you for such sound sleep as I enjoyed; and thank you for being with me in the wakeful periods. Thank you for safety, warmth and rest during the dark hours.

Lord, be with all those who face the day after a restless night: those who were harassed in their hearts by fears, angers or griefs; those who had to work all night when they were already weary; those who faced danger or suffering in the night; those who committed crimes in the night; those who were their victims; and those who in the night gave up life's struggle, for whom the morning opens in that life which is wholly yours and is one day to be mine.

Lord, take all that happened to so many in the night, redeem it, and use it for our good. I thank you, my Lord.

Lord, last night I made promises to myself and to you. Those intentions, Lord! They seemed so utterly inescapable and the only right way forward, and my heart was comforted in their truth and resolve. But in the clear light of today I find I'm the same 'me' with the same temptations . . .

So, Lord, take these true intentions and fill them with *your* energy and resolve. Give me the continuing will to live a little more in the way your love directs, rather than in the instinctive reactions of my own little-mindedness. So give me generosity of spirit today, Lord, the will to go the extra mile with people, especially when I don't feel like it; give me the will to reconciliation, and the words and actions – and the longings of the heart – that will make such irenic intentions effective. Close my mouth to all harsh words and angry responses, and if I can't be gentle of speech then let me be silent.

Lord, shape my good intentions today into practical living for you. And I thank you that what I cannot do for my own sake, you will enable me to do for yours. Amen.

Nineteenth Day • EVENING

Lord, for the years
your love has kept and guided,
urged and inspired us,
cheered us on our way,
sought us and saved us,
pardoned and provided:
Lord of the years,
we bring our thanks today . . .

Lord, for our world;
when we disown and doubt you,
loveless in strength
and comfortless in pain.
hungry and helpless,
lost indeed without you:
Lord of the world
we pray that Christ may reign.[41]

Lord, tonight I come to you in fullness of heart to thank you
for your presence with me today. Thank you that when I was
faced with not wholly easy situations, you were there. Thank
you that in that delicate conversation, you were there. Thank
you that in that difficult family encounter, you were there.
Thank you that in those decisions I had to make, you were
there. Lord, I recall all these things now, and lay them before
you gratefully: _____

Be there in all that flows from them, Lord: redeem anything
wrong in them and bless all that was good. And I thank you
for all the similar days of the past in which you have so 'kept
and guided, urged and inspired' me, and kept me in your
way.

But my Father, I cannot seek sleep tonight until out of this very sense of deep thanksgiving for your loving care of me, I can bring to you this ache in my heart for my world; this world which is *your* world, Lord God, but so largely doesn't know it. I look at my own nation, so far drifted from you that for many it is a matter of incredulity that anyone should seek God in matters important to them. And so as a people, 'getting and spending, we lay waste our powers'. So we are losing the richness of our faith inheritance for the little ones growing up among us. And more: we cannot engage in understanding with those communities and nations for whom obedience to *their* God is their motivating vision and dynamic.

And everywhere, too, across the world there is the struggle for power, murderous in its effects. And so the energy and combined resources that should be used to work together to tackle the problems of drought and famine and disease and the vast movements of refugees are used instead for military arms and action.

Lord, my world, my world . . . O Lord, forgive us; heal us; redirect us.

Lord, I feel so helpless: what can I do, Lord, what can I do, among peoples lost without you?

And you say to me: you can practise thanksgiving with all your heart for the Lord you know and have learned to trust. And out of that habit of heart you can speak and live as God's witnesser in this little part of the world where you have been set. And you can carry, without attempting to assuage it, the pain you feel for the world, as the price of the love you have yourself experienced, and daily experience, in your walk with your kind Lord. And you can act in that kindness to others, knowing that there, just there, God himself is at work. And you can remain unafraid. That is what you can do.

That is what, under your hand, I can do, Lord. Keep me faithful. Amen.

Twentieth Day • MORNING

Lord,
no one is a stranger to you
and no one is ever far from your loving care.
In your kindness watch over refugees and exiles,
those separated from their loved ones,
young people who are lost,
and those who have left or run away from home.
Bring them safely to a place where they belong
and help us always to show your kindness
to strangers and those in need.[42]

'No one is a stranger to you' . . . a prayer for our times, Father,
and one especially for all those of us comfortable in our secure
niche in life, unthreatened by the tides of homeless humanity
sweeping across so many places of the world. People who are
homeless in their own homeland through civil war, famine,
terror, political corruption and pitiless exploitation. People who
are treated as less than human by fanatical political ideolo-
gues who purge whole groups in the name of ethnic purity.
Little people, powerless people, jostled about in their own country
by bullying and cruel minor officials; or buried in a sea of
bureaucratic paper even where intentions are good. O Lord
God, we in our comfortable secure homes among those who
know and respect us need to pray this prayer. I, comfortable
and secure, need to pray this prayer today.

And in our own society, Lord, there are subtler forms of
the same estrangement. Those new to the neighbourhood or
the local community who find themselves less than warmly
treated. My new colleagues, Lord: have I done anything except
the courtesies to show they are not 'strangers' to me? The

wistful outsiders, in families and among friends; those acquaintances on the edge of friendship yet never quite being admitted as friends. Those who somehow can't find their niche in life and wander among us, never wholly accepted. And the youngsters trying out their identities and miserably feeling they don't fit anywhere. O Lord, I pray for all such as are known to me:

———

And you say to me, helplessness on our part is not an option. For in the end it is about a habit of the heart, is it not, my Lord God? I have myself received from you the experience of total acceptance, the gathering in to your care that brings me from the outside into the comfort and support of being 'at home' with you and yours. Solely through your grace I am no stranger.

And this means that I can never think 'stranger' in the same way again. For if they are not strangers to you, then how can they be to me, after what you have shown me? So how do I think of them, Lord? Not just those who are part of the normal changing scene of my life, but those about whom our society is so exercised: the desperate asylum-seekers risking life to get here; the economic migrants; the ethnic groupings at the other end of the area, those whose strong, even militant, religious faith challenges mine? What is in my heart about them, Lord? *Will it bear your scrutiny?* What do I say to our politicians about it? *Will that bear your scrutiny?* What do I say publicly by word and action and privately in the intimacy of my own home? *Will it bear your scrutiny, Lord God?*

O Lord God, forgive. O Lord God, give me courage to refuse to be a stranger. Amen.

Twentieth Day • EVENING

Leave it all quietly to God, my rescue comes from him
alone.

(Psalm 62.5, trans. Moffatt)

O my Lord God, I sometimes feel so sick at heart over the images
I see on my television screen, or what I read in the newspaper
or hear on the radio. My world seems so sick, Lord, and I so
helpless.

O my God, I bring to you the horror of the fanatical
nationalism that sweeps across the world, the religious and
ethnic hatreds and the terrible brutality that supports them.
Judge and Saviour, bless and strengthen, as you have in the
past, all who challenge religious or racial imperialism among
the nations by searching for an honourable peace; all who toil
to alleviate the suffering caused by sectarian or state terrorism;
all who labour to protect weaker religious or racial groups;
all who work ceaselessly to build bridges of understanding.

And, Lord God, help me not to leave this to others, but by
what I say and do and am to share the struggle, speak your truth
amid the distortion of events, and in my heart grieve for the
suffering.

O my God, I bring to you the disarray of my own nation,
our gathering violence, our promiscuity, our selfishness, our
failure to live up to the ideals we publicly proclaim, and above
all our national loss of knowledge of you, and our moral
confusion. Judge and Saviour, bless and strengthen, as you
have in the past, all who work here to protect the vulnerable;
all who seek to control and assuage violence; all who challenge
selfishness as an acceptable philosophy of life; all who work to
redeem the political life of this country; all who seek, by word

82

and deed, to share you with a nation that largely does not know you.

And, Lord God, help me not to leave this to others, but by what I do and say and am to share the struggle, grieve with those who suffer or are near despair, and speak out not only your truth but your love.

Dear Lord, when I ponder these things I am shaken by distress and frustration. Help me to use all my best energies in the fight against the corrosion of your world; and having done so, to rest my soul quietly in trust that the outcome is in your hands, and I may safely leave it there. Amen.

Twenty-first Day • MORNING

A Julian contemplation

Be silent.
Be still.
Wait before your God.
　　Say nothing:
　　Ask nothing:
　　Be still.
Let your God look upon you.
　　That is all.
　　God knows.
　　God understands.
God loves you with an enormous love.
God only wants to look upon you with love.
　　Quiet.
　　Still.
　　Be.
Let your God love you.[43]

Keep me still, Father.

　　. . .

'Enormous love', Father?

　　. . .

You 'look upon *me*', Father?

　　. . .

O Lord God, I open my heart. Here _____
　　　　　Love me, Lord. Amen.

Middle-class blues

The man who has everything is far from secure . . .
What he is afraid of most
and what keeps him tossing some nights
on the electric under-blanket
listening to the antique clock
clicking with disapproval from the landing,
Are the stories that begin:
   He had everything
   A beautiful young wife
   A comfortable home
   A secure job,
   And then one day . . .[44]

'Then one day . . .' Lord, what am *I* afraid of most? Is it the threat
in that so well known story, of the fall of the comfortable,
the disaster that strikes unexpectedly at noon?

Yes, I *do* fear what life's twists and turns of circumstances
can do, Lord. But I have a deeper fear than that.

The darkest fear I have is the loss of my sense of your purpose in things. However overwhelming the surge and suck of the
great tides, however intense the battering of events, the sense
of your grip, Lord, has steadied me.

But one day, I know, I could lose that sense that ultimately
you are in charge. So it is for many; so it was for the Lord Jesus,
crying out aloud the worst agony of all: 'My God, my God, why
have you forsaken me?'

Lord God, that is what I am afraid of most. That is what
so many of us fear more than anything: the loss of the sense

of your sovereignty. Which doesn't mean we are free from fear of the other smaller disasters implied in the words, 'And then one day . . .' Just that they are less absolute than that ultimate pain.

Lord Jesus, you taught us to pray, 'Do not bring us to the time of trial, but deliver us from evil'. So tonight I pray it.

Not just for myself, but for those especially dear to me. Here I name them _____

And not just for them, but for all those who this night are seizing up with anxiety, fear, dread. Here I bring them to you _____

Deliver us from evil:
The evil of losing your way for our life;
The evil of losing faith in you.

Lord, I thank you for teaching me that prayer. Fulfil it, Lord. Amen.

An African elegy

We are the miracles that God made
To taste the bitter fruit of Time.
We are precious.
And one day our suffering
Will turn into the wonders of the earth . . .

There are secret miracles at work
That only Time will bring forth.
I too have heard the dead singing.

And they tell me that
This life is good
They tell me to live it gently
With fire, and always with hope.
There is wonder here

And there is surprise.
In everything the unseen moves.
The ocean is full of songs.
The sky is not an enemy.
Destiny is our friend.[45]

O God of miracle, thank you that in every age men and women have found the language to declare your miracle. Thank you that these lines of delight and affirmation were inspired by Africa, even in the midst of her current 'bitter fruit of Time': drought, dislocation, strife and poverty. Thank you that our today in the West, in spite of our cynicism and materialism, still recognizes and honours the authentic voice of the prophet. So today, Lord, help *me* to hear this voice and join in its affirmation:

Lord God, we are *the miracles you made.*
Here I affirm that mystery with wonder _____
Lord God, to you *we are precious,*
Here I affirm that mystery with surprise! _____
Lord God, all we endure will *one day turn into the wonders of the earth,*
Here I affirm that mystery with yearning faith _____
So let me take to myself now the certainty that there are secret miracles, your miracles, at work; may they touch today the lives of those most in need of comfort or vision.
Here I name those known to me _____

And so let me bind to myself the gentleness, the fire, the hope and wonder that is your gift, in faithful expectation that among us moves always your unseen. And your destiny for us, through whatever our times of darkness, steadily, unswervingly and infallibly, advances our good. Through Christ our Lord. Amen.

An evening prayer before winter's ending

Lord, I have been driving all day, and I am very tired.
This bleak wind has been blowing for weeks, Lord,
And for months the grey trees have mapped the grey
    sky;
And there are no mountains here.
I can't even dream mountains any more.
Just grey, mud-splashed plain,
And the thrumming and swishing of wet tyres
On the wet grey road.
The world is so flat, Lord. No form or shape or light
    to it.
No contour or perspective. No landmarks even.
Lightless grey above and under and round me.
Even dramatic darkness would be better than this.

Lord, I know you told me just to keep on driving
    steadily,
And one day the road would loop into the longed-for
    city.
But I don't seem to be getting anywhere. The same
    road
With the same bitter stunted hedges
For mile after mile after mile.

Lord, what if I've come the wrong way?
What if I've missed the turning you wanted me to take?
I get drowsy, Lord, and numbed, going on and on
    like this.
Supposing I've missed your road

And am pulsing steadily in the wrong direction?
No, I'm comfortable enough. Just miserable,
Because the road lacks definition, and it's so long
    since I saw a sign.
Lord, this is your car.
If this is how you want it, and this is where you want it,
Keep me awake, Lord, and give me a direction.

Child, they are there, in the distance,
But you cannot see the mountains for the murk.
The young shoots are there, in the future,
But masked from you by mud and last year's deadness.
You cannot see the city because you are not there yet.
– And it would be inappropriate to move it
Just to shorten your journey.
Yes, I know it's lightless and grey; what else could
    twilight be?
(Temperateness is torment to the intemperate.)
Before the modulations of the city a journey must
    be made,
Or the city's centre can't be reached.
But a sign? What need a sign, when the road goes
    straight,
Undeviatingly on, all side-turnings blocked?
What need a sign when the road's direction's clear?
You do not fear you are lost.
You are simply impatient to arrive.
I taught you to drive, child, and gave you the road.
All that matters is the journeying.
To travel faithfully
Is to arrive . . .

Yes, Lord, I hear you. Help me to keep on steadily making my
life's journey, even when it feels as though it's going nowhere

and hasn't known your blessed Spring sunshine for a long time. Help me trust, Lord, and so travel faithfully, that I arrive in your lovely city at last. And comfort all those who tonight are lost in the murk of life, and longing for a direction. Amen.

You shall go out with joy and be led forth with peace.
And the mountains and the hills shall break forth
　　before you,
There'll be shouts of joy and the trees of the field
Shall clap, shall clap their hands
And the trees of the field shall clap their hands
And you'll go out with joy.[46]

Hosanna! hosanna! hosanna! Thank you, Lord, for this hosanna hymn . . . Its melody rings in my ear as I repeat these words, its rhythm a true echo of the songs of your people right back through time, back to your first calling out of a community to love and follow you. O Lord God, thank you for this vision you give of your people at peace, delighting in a Creation restored, and the whole Earth and all that it inhabit shouting your praises with joy. It is no mere dream. It is a vision rooted in your promise, Lord God: and here I affirm the vision and claim the promise for my world and myself, that some time, in your own good time, dear Lord, we may see the promise fulfilled.

And meantime forgive, O forgive, all the offences I and my generation have committed against your Creation, raping the land, poisoning the seas and abusing the creatures. Help me to be ready not just to accept necessary life-changes, but to initiate them, in order to care better for the Earth.

As I pray that, Lord, I look at my life and ask myself what practical steps I am in fact taking? Here I name them and offer them to you _____

Lord, they are so little and cautious!
Forgive me that I am so defensive of self-interest, that
   what I do to bring nearer the marvellous day of this
   vision is so meagre and limited.
Help me be braver in this matter, Lord.
Help my generation to be braver.

Help our politicians to be braver, taking the long view instead
of a political short view. Help us not to be thrown into ineffective pessimism by the doom-mongers, or lured off-course by
the complacent; but trusting your promise, work with you in
those small areas that are our own personal responsibility.
Including the way we vote and the lifestyle we adopt.

   And praise, praise to you, Lord God, that your victory over
our sin against Creation is as assured as your victory over all
other sins by which we fall short of the glory you invite us to.
Through – let Earth shout it with joy! – through Jesus Christ
our Lord. Amen.

Twenty-third Day • EVENING

Lord God,
Bring your joy into all families,
strengthen and deliver those in childbirth,
watch over children and guide the young,
bring reconciliation to those in discord
and peace to those in stress.[47]

My family, Father God: tonight I want to bring my family to you, in thankfulness and in hope. All those who share this home at this time: in my mind I visit each room and ask the blessing of your joy on _____ and _____ and _____ within them. Watch over them and bless them, especially _____ who is struggling with so much, and _____ who has such dreams of the future. And thank you for your gift of them to me.

And I pray for my scattered family, Father God. Be present, be present with _____ whom I miss so much and long to see more often than is possible; and with _____ who is not happy. Lord God, guard them as I cannot; cheer them as I cannot; give them the wisdom I cannot. And may they discover more and more of the wonders of your care, loving Father, and find what it is to walk their way with you. And thank you for your gift of them to me.

And I thank you for the senior members of my family, some who have moved on from this world into the joy of your immediate presence, and some whose continued vigour and wisdom I rejoice in. Thank you for my mother and father, their care of me, and all I have learned through them. Thank you for others of their generation who have given me their affection and encouragement and understanding. Thank you for those who prayed for me from early childhood, whose unseen influence has helped shape my life. May they know an ever-increasing delight in your presence with them. And thank you for your gift of them to me.

And I thank you for those whom I think of as 'family' because they have drawn me into the intimacies of their circle and offered me family affection. Lord, I ask the wonder of your blessing on their generous hearts, and the sure defence of your hand on their lives. I remember especially _____ and _____. And thank you for your gift of them to me.

Finally, Lord, I bring to you those of whose vulnerability this Litany reminds us: those families where new lives are coming into the world, and completed lives are ending. Lord, be with all mothers in childbirth this night, and with those whose lives are approaching their close: may the deep calm of your grace surround and support their spirits in the mysterious struggles of life and death. And I pray for all who are this night struggling with discord in their hearts, especially any for whom I am myself in any way its cause. O my Lord Christ, draw us all into the astonishing sweetness of your reconciling power, that we may know ourselves forgiven and forgiving. Be with any of us for whom the general stress of life is robbing our peace: speak a quietness to us tonight, Father God, that we turn to you with a child's confidence, and in your sustaining presence, sleep. Under the gentle touch of Christ Jesus our Lord. Amen.

No sooner saved, nor of sincerer faith,
Than ploughmen and pasturers and common people,
Shoemakers and shepherds and simple jots as these
Pierce with a pater-noster the palace of heaven.
And pass purgatory penance-less at their hence-parting,
Into the bliss of paradise for their pure belief,
Imperfectly here as they knew and even lived.[48]

Not many of you were wise by human standards, not
many were powerful, not many were of noble birth . . .
But God chose what is low and despised in the world . . .
so that no one might boast in the presence of God. For
God's foolishness is wiser than human wisdom, and
God's weakness is stronger than human strength.

(1 Corinthians 1.26, 28–29, 25)

Lord God, here are two voices from our Christian predecessors, one from 2,000 years ago away on the shores of the Mediterranean, the other from a still recognizable England of 600 years ago; both reminding us in this cynical, sophisticated, success-oriented age of ours of that which is most to be honoured and cherished wherever we find it: 'pure belief', however imperfectly known or even lived.

Lord God, thank you for the ordinary humble men and women of faith who in the past have honoured you in simplicity of heart, whose successors I and my fellow believers now are. Keep me faithful, Lord, as they in their time were faithful, assailed as your followers are in every age by the doubts and temptations characteristic of the times. Lord Christ, I thank you for the present-day ordinary humble men and women who follow you, who live their lives unassumingly for you in the tasks in which they spend their days. 'Shoemakers and shepherds' among them still, Lord, but also secretaries and labourers, small traders and call-centre workers, shop assistants and refuse collectors, housewives and lorry drivers, care assistants and plumbers: all that huge army of workers who keep our collective show on the road; and among them your faithful ones who do it as for you. Thank you for what I have myself learned of you through their faith. And I pray for them now, that they may glimpse the true glory of the service they bring; and that your Church today may more fully honour and learn from them. For they walk in your footsteps, my Lord Christ the carpenter, and know you as only fellow workers can.

So go on teaching me, Lord, through them; and keep me listening. Amen.

Twenty-fourth Day • EVENING

Father . . .
keep us so close to Your heart
that even our dreams are peaceful,
and that we may see things . . .
more and more from your point of view.[49]

O loving and comforting Father, it has been such a hard day
that I could not stay focused on you. Help me now to come so
close to you that my foggy sight clears, and you are there, lucid
and loving in my life. So let me try to understand the bad bit
of the day in the light of your love.

Today, Father, I was badly wounded. People were not only
rude but hurtful, so that I felt battered and diminished and
misjudged. The pain of staying silent, Lord . . . And the misery
of not wholly managing to . . . And my anger and pain went on
darkening my day. And O, my Lord, as I tell you about it I feel
the tears from my sense of being wronged rising up within me.

Let me look at it again with the eyes of your love:

— You ask me, Lord, why does it matter so much that
  others misjudge me? – I *hurt*, Lord!

— Is it perhaps *not* my passion for justice that makes
  me weep, but my tender sensitivity about my own
  standing? – Yes, Lord, true, Lord. But still I mind . . .

— You ask me, Lord, do I think that God thinks less of
  me because of what was said? – No, Lord, the reverse.
  But still I grieve . . .

100

— You ask me, Lord, do I know that you love me? And that every struggle on my part to follow Christ's way in the face of unkindness or misunderstanding is a source of deep and loving joy to you? That Heaven is the richer for my struggles today? That today I entered just a little more into the fellowship of generous and selfless love whose name is discipleship and whose heart is the Cross?

— The Cross . . . I am ashamed of my grief. For yes, my Lord, I look at it and *know* you love me; and as I look at you when I say that, I know nothing in life or death matters more than that. The wounds remain: but, salved by you, their destructive bitter pain is gone. O my Lord, stay like this, lucid and loving, in my heart tonight.

Amen.

God of our ancestors,
I lie down without food,
I lie down hungry,
although others have eaten and lie down full.
Even if it be but . . . a little rock-rabbit,
give me, and I shall be grateful. I cry to
God, Ancestor of my ancestors. Amen.[50]

Lord, I need to pray this prayer with and for the starving of the world, much more often than I do. Forgive me for heedlessness: thank you that this prayer sharply reminds me that hunger is real and terrible and across the globe millions suffer it and die because of it. And millions have cried out to you in their suffering, God of their ancestors; and I know that your response to that cry, God of all our ancestors, can come *through me and those like me.* The many who 'have eaten and lie down full'.

Have I thanked you for the wonder of that simple fact, Father God? That I never know hunger as suffering, only as a pleasant sauce to the meal I eat? And as now I kneel and make my thanks to you for sustenance throughout my life, I ask you to make me more consistently prepared to do all I can to find for others my equivalent of that 'little rock-rabbit', to assuage the terrible hunger of those starving even while I have eaten and been satisfied.

And Lord, help me to be practical about this. Help me to spot the action that would start to change things: whether it's giving (till it hurts) to appeals, or sharing in the shoe-box charities, or working with local projects here or where the need is greatest. But also guide me in challenging anything in our western lifestyle that contributes to the poverty and consequent starvation of those in other parts of the world. And I know that includes the impact our way of life is making on the global climate, with its consequent floods and droughts, devastating the living conditions of so many. Remind me constantly that I make a difference – small though it is – and therefore it must be the right sort of difference. Because I can, I must.

And send that child of yours a little rock-rabbit today, Father: if necessary, through me. Amen.

> Blind unbelief is sure to err
>   And scan his works in vain;
> God is his own interpreter,
>   And he will make it plain.[51]

Lord, I have struggled so long, and I cannot find sense in it: so much terrible suffering in your world; so much wicked cruelty unchecked; so many innocent lives blighted or maimed by disease, war, famine, violence, greed, sectarian or ethnic hatred, natural disaster or the predatory forces of survival; or by sheer casual human selfishness. Lord, the bad prosper; and innocent ones suffer.

Lord, I cannot bear it. And I cannot bear that you allow it.

And then I look at you again, Lord, and I see
— not the all-powerful King in glory
— not the mighty Creator of the Universe,
But you, Lord,
— misunderstood by your closest friends
— betrayed by one you had a right to trust
— seized and manacled and hustled
— spat on and struck and flogged
— publicly stripped and humiliated
— strung up tight on an agonizing cross
— dying of thirst, heat, suffocation, shock, exhaustion
    and agony . . .
Lord, the bad prospered, and the innocent one suffered.

And you took it into yourself, and showed us indestructible life, indestructible love, more powerful and more glorious than any prosperity among the bad. Help me, Lord, always to prefer your way to your enemies' way, your cross to their triumph. And challenge me, sharply, to *trust*, as you did; to trust that somewhere, somehow, God will interpret all things for me – as you did on that Emmaus road – *and that he will make it plain.*

So give me faith and love till I have sight, Lord. Amen.

Twenty-sixth Day • MORNING

> Give me humility . . .
> If thou, Lord, hadst travelled in a
> sedan chair, how would the woman
> have touched thy garment's hem?[52]

Humility, Lord: not the false and self-pleasing unctuous servility of a Uriah Heep, but the costly real thing. O highest and holiest Lord, who chose willingly to share the narrowness and frailty and frustrations of our human life, teach me this 'real thing', the humility the apostle Paul talked of, which has nothing servile about it, which is not so much a series of actions as an attitude of heart, and which we can learn only from you.

> Let the same mind be in you that was in Christ Jesus,
> who, though he was in the form of God,
> > did not regard equality with God
> > as something to be exploited,
> but emptied himself,
> > taking the form of a slave,
> > being born in human likeness.
> And being found in human form,
> > he humbled himself
> > and became obedient to the point of death –
> > even death on a cross.
>
> *(Philippians 2.5–8)*

Help me never to travel in the spiritual equivalent of a sedan chair, Lord, protected from the crush and stress of human contact at other people's expense, or savouring a spurious sense of status. So what does that mean for my life? It means availability, and therefore vulnerability. Availability of my heart and my attention, and therefore of my time and energy. It means being vulnerable to feel the pain of others, their woundedness, their anger; sometimes, Lord, the evil they fondle and do not want to surrender, which I must face with them. It means time vulnerable to others' demands, when my real desires are for my own preferred activity, or for rest. It means energy available to the hunger of others, who are energized by it or feed on it or rest in it.

Lord, I realize that I cannot possibly manage any of that, can't manage without that spiritual sedan chair, unless it is *you* who are vulnerable in my heart, *you* who order my time, *you* who supply my energy. So be with and in me today, Lord Jesus, so that no rituals of pride or status or ease cut me off from being the means by which someone, in their need, can touch the hem of your garment. In your grace, Lord. Amen.

Twenty-sixth Day • EVENING

Prayer (Romans 8.26–28)

Desires fall away when you are near,
Except the one which is to be with you.
The heart is filled with love that casts out fear
And there is only one thing left to do;
Utter the single sound the soul can make,
Filled to the brim with what it can't contain,
Opening blinded eyes made clear awake,
And tasting sweetness after so much pain.

Power that brings the soul into your care,
Moved on the waters, moves now in the heart,
And now there's nothing else for me but prayer
Not knowing what to say, but keen to start.
By praying prayer that I cannot express,
By coming to you in my nothingness.[53]

We do not know how to pray as we ought . . . and that's the sum of it, Lord. I know that to be with you, mindful of you, focused on you, is my best and happiest state. I know that anything I can do for the world that is of enduring value depends on the impetus and sustaining that comes from your presence in my heart, and my attention to you. And yet so often I jib at spending the time and energy: things await action, people await response, life awaits living. And so, pushed by unnecessary urgencies, I leave this place of waiting on you before I should.

But when I take time, Lord, even then I do not know how to pray as I ought. Why? Because I try to do it myself, Lord. Because I try to follow my own agenda, raise myself to Heaven by my own trampolining. And all the time your gentle Holy Spirit is waiting, constant, for me to let go of my own striving and let *him* pray in me and for me. How I envy Peter when Jesus tells him he has prayed for him! The wonder of being prayed for by my Lord, the Son of God! And here you are reminding me that such prayer is available to each of us, all the time. All we have to do is to offer our longing hearts as available to him.

So, Lord, here I am before you: I set aside all the urgencies with which I came; I set aside all thoughts of my own condition and hope; I even set aside my own take on the world's condition and needs. Here I am, Lord. Accept this ineffective, stumbling heart and pray in it with those sighs that cannot be uttered.

Now, Lord . . . Here, Lord.

Pray in me, Spirit of God, for those I love,
for my world in its needs and joys.
I lay before you all that I presently am
and that you created me to be:
Hold me in your power and stillness, my Lord.

I affirm your promise
That all things work together for good
for those that love God.
Amen.

> Surrender your rights
>   to another.
> Surrender your rights
>   to the other.
>
> Whether friend or foe
>   let them go:
> Christ is always
>   the other.[54]

Lord Christ, I cannot do it. I'm not even sure I ought to try. What about my proper self-respect? What about the integrity of my position? What about the exercise of right judgement, and the vindication of truth? Bluntly, Lord, how can it be right that those others *get away with it*?

No, Lord, I don't exactly want to call down fire from heaven on them. I do remember what you said to your disciples about that. It's just that if my rights are real (and I know that in you they are, because you are God of justice) then how can I properly let them be trampled on?

O my dear Lord, even as I protest I see the answer in your face and in your bleeding body. It's not the justice of the case, is it, Lord, but the mercy? Your mercy? It's thinking with a faint, faint shadow of your marvellously generous love about every being with whom I share the world, even if they are standing offensively on my patch? O Jesus, how can I begin to grasp your kind of loving? That concedes the demand, for love of the person making it. Your kind of loving, that even abandoned Heaven, your rightful place, so that we might share it with you.

So enlarge my heart, Lord, that I may truly begin to see others that way: as beings whose 'rights' I care for, even at the expense of my own. Let me see you, Christ, in each of them, beginning today. Amen.

Twenty-seventh Day • EVENING

You were here, and now you are not

There is nothing to compare with the pain of death.
You were here, and now you are not.
That's all.

I search for you in old photographs, letters,
things you touched
things that remind me of you,
but they cannot fill the space you occupied.

The space is *in* me, too,
bleeding round the edges where you were torn away.
In the night, strange shapes haunt the space . . .
regret, fear, fury,
all the things we might have done,
all the unused dreams.

How can I go on with this hole inside me?
A partial person?
God, don't let me fill the space with the wrong things.
Don't let me cover it up
to eat me from within.
Give me courage to bear my emptiness,
to hold it gently
till the edges stop bleeding;
(will they? ever?)
till the darkness becomes friendly;
till I see some star at its heart;
till it becomes a fertile space,
growing new life within it.

If we had not loved you, we would not have wept.
This love you have given us;
this love we have carried
this love has carried us.
And I know that though I cannot see you, touch you,
the love does not go away.[55]

Lord, I have my dead, too.
When I let myself think of them, then the ache returns.
For there *is* nothing to compare with the pain of loss,
whether by death or separation or breakdown in
   relationships.
Lord, I have my dead, too.
Here I remember them before you _____

And safe in your presence, help me uncover the pain of that loss and face it steadily. Am I filling that emptiness with the wrong things, or if the right things, in the wrong way? Show me, show me, Lord: and if I am, show me how not to. Help me, O help me to use my best memories of them to make their absence a fertile space within which you will nourish new life. For indeed, indeed, the love does not go away.

For the gift of that love, keep me thankful, Lord: to them and to you. Amen.

Thinking in terms of one
Is easily done –
One room, one bed, one chair,
One person there,
Makes perfect sense;
One set of wishes to be met,
One coffin filled.

But counting up to two
Is harder to do;
For one must be denied
Before it is tried.[56]

And the temptation is, Lord, in this individualistic, fragmented society I live in, to think only in terms of 'one': *oneself*. It's so easy to slip into the habit, and to be defensive about the life-style that grows from it.

Lord, forgive me my own lapses into self-centredness: some-times, I fear, they are more than lapses – they coalesce into a habit of heart. O Lord, help me fight them.

And thank you for those many who have refused to be seduced by self-accommodation, and have opened their hearts and minds – and lives – to those around them. Thank you that I have met and been blessed by such in my life. Thank you that by their large-heartedness they have taught me the loveliness of generosity; by their care for others they have taught me the beauty of unselfish action; by their thoughtfulness they have shown me what it is to be aware.

Here in your presence with gratitude I name them ———

And if I am to learn to do likewise, then I must learn to deny myself not just occasionally but consistently, almost instinctively. Lord, it's too hard. I can't do it. If I'm honest, I can't do it . . . Without your help I can't do it.

So be with me as I try, and help me keep on trying.

For I know that the well-being of the world depends on ordinary people like me trying to walk the way of self-denial for others' sake. (And yours? . . .)

And I know that Heaven will only be Heaven if I have learned to *want it for other people* at least as much as for myself. For you, Lord, showed us the way to Heaven when you denied yourself its joys for our sake, bore the weight of Earth's burdens in the Cross on your shoulder, and so made footprints for us to follow heavenwards.

Only I can't tread them in my own strength, Lord.

So – whatever my family circumstances – be my Other, so that I always have to think in terms of Two.

For your love's sake. Amen.

Twenty-eighth Day • EVENING

O Lord God, as this month nears its end, I make this version
of Psalm 151 my own, in glory to you and with deep
thankfulness:

I am come, a long time after the event, to say that
God is here;
and not merely in the candlelit places, nor the souls of
the inspired, but in this street.
He is running like the winter, like the rain along
this street.
He is dancing with the leaves in the gutter.
He is in the music of the elderly tramp, blowing and
gasping on the wet and windy corner. He is in the
bobbing masses moving unconsciously to the rhythm
of the music.
He is trembling with the trees, with the sky mirrored
in the shop window; he is entwined around the
railings of the yard where scrap is sold.
He is hidden in the averted faces of the crowds as
they shuffle along the street with down-turned vision.
He is the new grass parting the concrete, and the artistry
of a snail.
Oh the Lord is in me and may not be measured.
Within the convoluted folds of this raincoat, I am
extended inwards in all infinity.
In the wet blue darkness the car lamps shine, and are
captured by the myriad drops of rain, and the running
streams of water on the pavement.
Each lamp reflects the light of the sun, and is in turn
reflected by the shop windows, which are reflected in
other shop windows, and so on world without end.

So the Lord makes his face to shine upon me, and
   leads me to the places of light.
Glory be to the stars, and to the beetles, and to his holy
   substance:
Which, as it was in the beginning, is now and ever shall
   be. Amen.[57]

There have been times
when, after long on my knees
in a cold chancel, a stone has rolled
from my mind, and I have looked
in, and seen the old questions lie
folded in place
by themselves, like the piled
grave-clothes of love's risen body.[58]

O lovely moment! Dear Lord, that wonderful moment you give just now and then when I *know* resurrection: know that life, your life, is unquenchable. And you gently put aside all the questions, doubts, fears, like unnecessary grave-clothes that have wrapped up my mortality, no longer needed *because mortality is not the final condition.*

That's the 'Good News', Lord, that you came to share with us. That indeed you came to make happen . . .

Beyond any other possibility, that is the Good News about life. And it's good news not just about *my* future but about other people's. About your glorious Creation and all that it inhabit. O Lord, that is the ultimate joy of it. Let me lose myself in wonder in those moments when suddenly I grasp it again.

And now, knowing the truth of those glimpses, I bring to you all the times when my prayers have been cold, and felt unblessed; all the times when my prayers have been confused and muddled about the day's small concerns and trifles; all the times when I simply haven't prayed at all, lacking conviction or energy.

And you waited patiently, Lord. Until that lovely moment when, body, heart, mind and soul in accord, I was open to you, no questions left: and there I glimpsed your radiant life and knew that you shared it with me and mine.

Lord, in the many, many days when the stone blocks my soul, and questions, doubts, anxieties, preoccupations dominate it: on those days stay with me, an unseen, unfelt presence. And forgive my frailty and bless my longing. Amen.

Twenty-ninth Day • EVENING

I do not know
what resurrection is
(though I'm almost sure
it has something to do
with hallowing common ground) . . .

I expect one day I'll get up
and find that it sneaked up on me
while I wasn't looking
and maybe even that it's been there all along . . .

In the meantime
I believe in it.[59]

O great, all-holy and most loving God, thank you for today. Thank you for everything in it that has hallowed the common ground of my life. Thank you for your gift of prayer, with which the day began, and in which you took charge of the hours ahead. Thank you for the fellow pilgrims I met as I went about my affairs, and our exchanges in your presence. Thank you for the freedom here to speak and practise the faith you have inspired: for public worship and private devotions and shared experiences of your hand upon us even amid my ordinary daily doings. Forgive me that sometimes I take that freedom for granted and am even careless of the gift, especially of public worship, when others in other places die for their faithfulness. Thank you for all words, music and art that inspire, and thank you too for the food for my soul in the Bible and thoughtful, even astringent, books about how better to know you. Thank you for others' shared reflections on their journey with you. Thank you for all the ordinary happenings of the day when I glimpsed you and knew the day holy.

And now, Father, as I turn to my rest, let me grasp afresh that you have made me for eternity and I live my life in its light. And so, as I think of tomorrow, and prepare myself for sleep tonight, let me know Christ's resurrection power afresh, whether sleeping or waking, at leisure or work-burdened.

And may my life in pilgrimage, through this ground you have hallowed for me, be a song of resurrection praise. Amen.

Thirtieth Day • MORNING

'Father, if you are willing, remove this cup from me; yet, not my will but yours be done.'

(Luke 22.42)

Lord, I'm frightened. When I let myself look at this thing I've got to face, I'm frightened. Most of the time I try to put it out of my mind, but I know it's lurking there, whispering to me. And I know at some point I've got to turn and face it and give it my full attention. Because though I keep hoping the worst can be avoided, I know that almost certainly it can't. And then I feel sick, and tremble within, and shiver; and I know fear.

I think, Lord Jesus, if you hadn't made this experience your own, I'd be in danger of totally panicking. But you've been there: in Gethsemane, in Gethsemane – O how grateful I am that you went through Gethsemane for me. Because you faced there something much worse than I do. For you could so easily have swept aside the tormenters you knew were coming for you: there was no *must* for you. If it happened, it did so because you *chose for our sake to let it.* You chose to accept it – for love of us – with all the authority and dignity of one who could have made it quite other. And that must have added to the intensity of that fearful anticipation in the Garden. So you sweated in the night over it, as I do. You sweated. So that it was like great drops of blood dripping . . . what *extreme* of anguish of mind showed itself in that, my Lord.

So I know you are here in this experience ahead that I'm so dreading, and that I can hold on to you, tight, all the way through. Be with me, my Lord: remind me constantly of your presence right there in the middle of it all, at my side. And give me the courage I don't have: give me the will to ask you for it when

I most need it, and the trust to be quite sure you will give it to me. And keep me open to all the help you send through your human messengers, and through the beauty of this lovely world of yours which is mine daily.

And stay with me, Lord Christ, right through to the end; so that I can join in with your 'It is finished', knowing you, and you only, have brought me through to completion. For in you I trust. In you I hope. In you is my life. Amen.

Thirtieth Day • EVENING

Lord, in this blessed quietness, I rest my spirit on these great
hymns of your peace:

> Christ, my Beloved, which still doth feed
> Among the flowers, having delight
>   Among the faithful lilies,
> Doth take great care for me indeed
> And I again with all my might
>   Will do what so his will is.
>
> My Love in me and I in him,
> Conjoined by love, will still abide
>   Among the faithful lilies
> Till day doth break, and truth do dim
> All shadows dark, and cause them slide
>   According as his will is.[60]

My God and my Lord, eyes are at rest, stars are setting,
hushed are the movements of birds in their nests . . . And
thou art the just who knowest no change, the equity
that swerveth not, the everlasting that passeth not away.
The doors are locked . . . But thy love is open to him who
calls on thee. My Lord, each lover is now alone with his
beloved. Thou for me art the beloved One.[61]

May He support us all the day long, till the shades
lengthen, and the evening comes, and the busy world is
hushed, and the fever of life is over, and our work is done.
Then in His mercy may He give us a safe lodging, and a
holy rest, and peace at the last. Amen.[62]

O my Lord Love, whose equity swerves not, gather me tonight into your peace at the heart of things, that I rest in utter confidence in the One who, as days come and go, knows no change; and so keep me safe and holy, tonight and always. Amen.

Thirty-first Day • MORNING

Two friends pass a cemetery gate on which are engraved Hebrew characters. One of them translates:

> 'It says, "Born, mankind is doomed to die. Dead, mankind is destined to live again." '
> We walked on.
> 'Grace: . . . Oliver Cromwell fought his hardest battles for it. A crowning mercy . . .'
> 'I don't believe,' I said, 'that grace has to be fought for. I believe it's there for the asking.'[63]

'I believe it's there for the asking' . . . Grace, in which the whole Creation is sustained; grace, which shapes all your divine dealings with us, Lord; grace, personal and universal, redeeming and transforming my own life and seeking to draw all humanity to you in love. And it's there for the asking . . . Your gift, your gift, your *gift*. Through dreadful disaster and joyous celebration alike, the golden glint of your grace shines in our world.

But we make such a labour of it for ourselves, Lord, constantly flogging ourselves to deserve it. (As if we could!) So as this month ends, let me in wondering thankfulness accept the gift of your grace as I have known it in these weeks, and shall know it, trusting in your promise, for all time and beyond time:

> There's a wideness in God's mercy
>   like the wideness of the sea,
> there's a kindness in his justice
>   which is more than liberty.
>
> There is no place where earth's sorrows
>   are more felt than up in heaven;

there is no place where earth's failings
   have such kindly judgement given.

There is plentiful redemption
   in the blood that has been shed;
there is joy for all the members
   in the sorrows of the head.

For the love of God is broader
   than the measures of man's mind;
and the heart of the Eternal
   is most wonderfully kind.

If our love were but more simple
   we should take him at his word;
and our lives would be all sunshine
   in the sweetness of the Lord.[64]

Concerning the builder of an ancient cathedral – dead 800 years

> He knew that right
> building was a moral force, that
> stone can grow . . . A plain man
> building in faith . . . he saw
> the miracle which is not a swift
> visitation, nor an incredible
> suspension of the commonplace,
> but the church grown great about us,
> as if the first stone was a seed.[65]

'Right building is a moral force': whether in stone or lives.

Lord, thank you for the great cathedrals built in faith.

Through the ages all across the world, they stand as signals of your presence among us, and direct us always to Heaven. Thank you for the faith that maintained their slow progression towards completion. Thank you that for each generation they are never wholly complete, for always there is work to be done in faith, for present ministry and the inspiration of generations to come. Thank you for the ages of prayer they have inspired and sustained and sheltered. And thank you for the scars these ancient buildings bear, which mark the woundedness and sin of our humanity, and our need for that miracle of your intervention told of and celebrated here daily.

Lord, thank you for the great cathedrals built in faith.

Yet more, Lord, thank you for all the 'right building' you sustain of your Church.

Of that company of believers through space and time whose lives and worship you have built stone by stone into a living fabric witnessing to your grace and unfailing love, through joy and disaster, through periods of wandering astray and times of rediscovering your Way for your people.

> Lord, forgive the wounds and blemishes that scar your living Church through our wrongdoing and wrong understanding:
> Lord, help us to see in such scars a guide and warning for the future:
> Lord, help us to accept those scars that come from faithful witnessing in a rejecting world, as reminders of the wounds you yourself bore in your body.
>   For us.
>   For me.

And so Lord, I thank you for your 'right building' of that small cathedral, my life.

Thank you for those foundations laid down long before I could myself make choices. Thank you that I have known the 'swift visitation', but also known the greatest miracle, the slow, purposeful, stone-by-stone growing towards your design; learning in company with others the baptizing and redeeming of the commonplace so that it becomes holy to you. Forgive the wounds and blemishes in this little cathedral that came from my own waywardness. Thank you that like the scarred stones of the ancient buildings they too can speak of the beauty of your grace.

Dear Lord, make my little cathedral a place of hospitality, where prayer is constant and your love a holy and unfailing presence. Till its completion. Amen.

Seasonal supplement for LENT, PALM SUNDAY, HOLY WEEK, EASTER, ASCENSION DAY, PENTECOST and TRINITY SUNDAY

Prologue

My cross is a rainbow-coloured cross,
Violet, Indigo, Blue, Green, Yellow, Orange, Red,
Colours of the rainbow . . .

My cross is a rainbow-coloured cross,
For I am blue with the pain of oppression
Indigo with the struggle for freedom
And green with hope.

As I walk the royal (violet) road of liberation
With flowers yellow, orange and red,
Springing up in celebration
Of new life,
Creating a new Spring
Of eternal liberation
In the Resurrection of Christ.[66]

I'm hunting rainbows, Lord. Not 'somewhere at the end of', that synthetic dream of elusive pots of gold, never to be discovered as the rainbow's end melts ever before us. That fantasy feeds no folk, nor ever will. But there are rainbows in my life, Lord, that sign me something more wonderful than any lottery jackpot of rainbow-coloured balls.

So help me see the colours of your Cross in the hard things I know I may have to face, as I make this Easter journey, and the painful jolts that so often come unexpectedly all through life. Is there the indigo of tough struggle ahead? Or a blue bullying to be borne, even if only verbal, even if only oblique, even if ever so polite in its manipulativeness? There stands your rainbow Cross; and there you make holy my struggle to bear these things patiently through your grace. And green around it peep the new shoots of living hope, promising a blessing to come.

Help me loose just one small part of the life I encounter from whatever imprisons or burdens it, and so I walk the royal violet road of liberation: even if it's simply doing a sick neighbour's shopping, or refusing to use my vote simply for my own advantage.

Royal violet of my Lord's Cross, be discovered right there in every free act of service. And let me glory in your colours of celebration, yellow, orange, red, in every small victory of order over chaos, kindness over harshness, the irenic word that dissolves dispute in place of the angry retort that fuels it. Let me recognize in such moments, my Lord Christ, that sovereignty to which you ascended: the Lord whom every created being shall honour. And let me acknowledge the sweeping power of your Holy Spirit, alive and at work among us since Pentecost. Alive and at work in my own life, and that of a million others, today. O rainbow Christ, be discovered in and make holy my life today, and in whatever lies before me in the future. In your name and power, Lord God who created the rainbow, reminding us that you love us; and save us. Amen.

Ash Wednesday

Rag-and-bone confession

There are lumps under our carpet
that the Hoover won't help

There are cats tied in bags
would be off like a flash

Skeletons in the cupboards
tap tap on the doors

There is nothing hidden
but that's going to get out
So let's get it over with, God.

There's a pile at the foot of the Cross
of the things we could do without.

Make us glad we brought them
to you who carry away
the sins of the world
and grant in their place
pardon and grace
and your call to be following always.[67]

O my Lord, the rag-and-bone man of our lives, carrying away
what we want to get rid of and *paying* for it, dear Lord, let me
now acknowledge the lumps of things swept under my carpet,
the skeletons in my cupboard – some, perhaps, I haven't faced
in a long time.

Lord, I bring to you
all that I did wrong yesterday and have already
done today

all that I did wrong this week
all the thinking and feeling and habit of mind
that lay behind them.
Lord, I bring to you
that temptation I have struggled with so long,
and failed to conquer
that desire that is out of control
that long-term relationship that is in a mess
that ambition that is self-promoting
that fearfulness that makes me a coward
that doubt that stops me going all the way
with you.

O loving and gracious Lord Jesus, I thank you that you are willing to take all these – and my secret and whispering sins, my Lord – from my back; and will go on doing so because you love me.

See, I pile them up at the foot of your Cross
— those wrong actions
— that way of thinking and feeling
— those desires, relationships, ambitions, fears,
bitternesses that clog my life today.
In faith I thank you that you *have* taken them and dealt with them.
Strengthen me in the certainty of what you have done
And let me go out today in gladness
as your loved and forgiven child
To share that amazing love
with your loved and forgiven world.
Amen.

Lent 1

Lambs that learn to walk in snow
Where their bleating clouds the air
Meet a vast unwelcome, know
Nothing but a sunless glare.
Newly stumbling to and fro
All they find, outside the fold,
Is a wretched width of cold.

As they wait beside the ewe,
Her fleece wetly caked, there lies
Hidden round them, waiting too,
Earth's immeasurable surprise.
They could not grasp it, if they knew
What so soon would wake and grow
Utterly unlike the snow.[68]

'Earth's immeasurable surprise' . . . more amazing every year, Lord. Even as one thinks of it, in this chilly fag-end of the winter, it seems beyond realization: though the current shouting of the birds in the cold dawn insists it is coming, it is coming. Lord, thank you for the marvellous yearly surprise of Spring, for its forerunners the fragile snowdrops pushing their frail green stems through the hard earth; for the vivid hyacinths unclenching their brilliant curled fists of colour; for, most of all, the gallant gold of the daffodils shaking their defiant heads in the sleety winds.

But there's much, much more to all this, isn't there, Lord? For *we* are your lambs, learning to walk in snow and stumbling through much of our lives in what quite often feels a vast unwelcome, a wretched width of cold. And so we cannot grasp (even though we have been told of it) Heaven's immeasurable surprise awaiting us, waking and growing around us – and *in* us. To break upon our astonished and wondering eyes in the full brilliance of that glory that Earth foretells, which is the warm, gladdening light of Heaven's eternal summer; for us to delight in, among the sweet meadows in which you will pasture us for ever.

O Lord, for all the surprises – the immeasurable surprises – ahead of us in your love: thank you. Thank you. Amen.

Lent 2

So I turned and went down from the mountain . . . the
two tablets of the covenant were in my two hands. Then
I saw that you had indeed sinned against the LORD your
God, by casting for yourselves an image of a calf . . . So
I flung the two tablets from my two hands, smashing them
before your eyes. Then I lay prostrate before the LORD as
before, for forty days and forty nights; I neither ate bread
nor drank water . . . I prayed to the LORD and said, 'Lord
GOD, do not destroy the people who are your very own
possession . . .' At that time the LORD said to me, 'Carve
out two tablets of stone like the former ones, and come up
to me on the mountain . . . I will write on the tablets the
words that were on the former tablets . . .'

(Deuteronomy 9.15–10.2)

Jesus, full of the Holy Spirit, returned from the Jordan
and was led by the Spirit in the wilderness, where for
forty days he was tempted by the devil. He ate nothing
at all during those days, and when they were over, he was
famished. The devil said to him, 'If you are the Son of
God . . .'

(Luke 4.1–3)

You are on a high, Lord. Your calling and very identity have
been confirmed not just in your heart but publicly at the river
Jordan. And at that moment of glorious certainty you are
swept off to the lonely place of privation, to face the deepest
uncertainty of human life, the uncertainty we all face: how to
be who we are, rightly and fulfillingly.

But there's far more to it than that, isn't there, Lord? Your life is repeating the experience of God's earlier messengers. Moses wrestled with God on the wild mountain for 40 days and nights, to create the Law that would make his wanderers a nation, a people of God. Then they went desperately astray and it was all to do again. So he spent *another* 40 days and nights fasting and praying to save them from their deserved fate. And out of that, at last, the Law was established that still underlies many of our present society's values. So when you, my Lord Jesus, were 'tested' while fasting for 40 days, it was not about your own proper way forward. That came at the end. Those 40 days of being tried were about the new Law of God *for your people*: what its nature should be. The new Law of God's Love as we were to know it and live it.

The grief of Moses over his erring people as he lay prostrate, was that a grief you too knew then, as you showed it later weeping over Jerusalem? Was that 40 days of wrestling in the wilderness not only a time of discovering, in your self-denying dialogue with the Father God, the new Law of Love, but also its price tag? As with Moses, the costly setting of yourself between the sin and its consequences, the sinner and the Judge. Did you pour out your soul in anguish as Moses had, pleading for a way through for your people who do not deserve a way through? And God showed it to you. And so finally it was only the *means* of our saving to be determined – the three temptations at the end of it all. And you put them steadily to one side in favour of their alternative: obedience to the Lord God – costing not less than everything. Then you spent your life – and your death – *showing* us the new Law of Love that God had incised on humanity, in you, for ever. Now I see what those 40 days in the wilderness were about; and your glorious resurrection showed how profoundly rightly they had shaped your ministry. The new Law of Love was in place, and your people's way to safety and the new life made secure.

O my Lord, help me too, in my Lenten time, to face the grief that goes with caring about the people to whom I belong. Lead me to the point where I am ready to pay the cost of standing between sinner and judgement, interceding, interceding, interceding, by deed and word and thought, for the people whose life and erring I share. My nation, Lord God! And the local community here. My Church, Lord God! And the local congregations here. In the name of my Lord Jesus Christ, who was tempted as we are, yet without sin. Amen.

Lent 3

At a time of national celebration of our history: a prayer about my nation

The 8th of May. This is the day that, some sixty years ago, the 'Allies' celebrated the relief and wonder of Victory in Europe: the black threat of Nazi totalitarianism was (at least for a time) gone. Overwhelmingly we felt that it was the Lord's doing, and marvellous in our eyes. But, Lord, how have we used that 'redemption'? Sixty years on, what have we built on it?

One of our poets wrote, for a first Remembrance Day Service of the new Millennium:

Once we had dreams, dreams of a new beginning,
when we had fought the war to end all war,
a world of peace, where people live in freedom,
a world where justice reigns for evermore.
And yet, and yet, each year as we remember
we know too well how subtly dreams can fade.[69]

Lord, I was a child of VE Day:
a teenager (just), full of unquestioning
patriotic certainties of joy.
Of course we won. You, God, were 'on our side'.
(And certainly you gave us moral courage, for at least
the evil we fought was clear and unquestionable.
There was Lucifer
arrogantly making the world his concentration camp.)

But now older, I look back and wonder
at the way we travelled like Bunyan's pilgrims
facing Apollyon, facing the lion,
facing the weasel words of doubters.
(Though Vanity Fair was no problem, in a land of
utility goods,
ration books and clothing coupons.)
Somehow, though, with all our sins on our heads
(the firestorm of Dresden still flickers in our hearts,
and the sickening glory of Hiroshima),
somehow you brought us, Lord, through
the terrible blackness creeping over the globe,
the chaining of freedom in torture cells,
to a sort of peace, to a chance to build anew
with an open vision, in a peace potential.

But now, Lord, I look back 60 years and grieve.
What have we done with your gift of freedom, Lord?
Your gift of Passover and the Red Sea crossed again
in our own generation?
For since you brought us out of slavery, and the bondage
of brute force . . . *we have sought retail therapy.*
We stopped off in Vanity Fair and have been there
ever since.

O forgive us, forgive us, my Lord, that we have preferred
Vanity Fair to our Promised Land.
And if need be, send such angels of fire and terror
as may once again shake us from our self-indulgences;
and raise again for us a Moses
who will destroy our Golden Calf and shock us with
your words;

till we stumble again into a wilderness that is yours
and find our feet again on the road, the right road,
the right road to your Promised Land.

For as the nations must answer to you, O Lord,
we need again your redemption from a subtler foe
than we have faced before. For now Lucifer is a dealer,
and we have made his supermarkets our temples . . .
'Hark to the ring of his bells!'

Lord God, I bring to you my nation and my own part in what
we have become. Forgive us, challenge us, purge us and save
us. That Christ be not crucified once more, this time in the
supermarkets. Or be sold as a commodity on the Internet.

In your great mercy, Father God, deliver us. Amen.

Lent 4 or Passion Sunday

Were you there when they crucified my Lord?
Were you there? . . .
O sometimes it causes me to tremble, tremble, tremble,
Were you there when they crucified my Lord?[70]

Lord, was I there?

Am I there among your disciples who flee? In the face of threat or mockery or humiliation, have I been, am I now, among those who back down from my belief, or deny my friendship, or run away?

Sometimes, Lord, it causes me to tremble, tremble, tremble . . .
Lord, was I there?

When they drag you through the city, am I there? One of an unthinking crowd, seeking the entertainment of public spectacle, thoughtless and heartless? Or judging and persecuting someone whom the group has made a victim; or silent while others do? Assenting to the majority view from fear or a desire to be in with the crowd, instead of obeying my conscience? Am I there, Lord?

Sometimes, Lord, it causes me to tremble, tremble, tremble . . .
Lord, was I there?

With those who love you, grieving beneath the Cross? Am I there? As they support each other, and suffer with you, am I there? Let me be there, Lord, trembling but there . . .

And may I be there with them, Lord, later, in dawning hope at the empty tomb; with them in astonished joy in the upper room; with them at Pentecost, crowned in the flame of your Spirit.

O Lord, the hope makes me tremble, tremble, tremble . . .
O Lord, may I be there. Amen.

Palm Sunday

Donkey

My mother told me
(When they sold me to their Jerusalem friend)
About the night everything changed.
A long time ago when she was very young.
After the journey (she carried Mary carefully,
Seeing her time was near)
They sheltered at last in a decent place
– The other beasts were welcoming,
Though it was crowded, my mother said –
And when at last they laid the baby in the straw
And everyone slept, then, my mother said,
Then, she said, and nuzzled my back as she told it,
The child opened his eyes and looked into hers.
Then she knew who he was, and the wonder.
So she rubbed his baby head, very gently,
With the softness of her nose. And somehow she knew
   from him
That the last foal she would bear would carry him
At some great moment to come.

Now she was old (they kept her long for love,
And because she carried them to Egypt;
After the kindness of shepherds, clumsily wondering,
And the great star through the rafters, and robed
   strangers
Smelling of strange things; after that they left
In a hurry, Mary and child and baggage
All piled on mother's back) . . .

Now she was old, and I to be sold,
Mature now, though her youngest,
To work for this friend in Jerusalem.
The great moment will come, she said,
And you will know him.

I never saw her again.
And now I too am ageing. But it happened as she said.
I had forgotten her tale, until last week,
When strangers came and loosed me from my stall.
(I was watching over a skittish young foal,
The mother being out at work.)
And they led me away to the top of the hill
Where he waited. He turned, looking into my eyes.
Then I knew who he was, and the wonder.
So I carried him carefully down the hill
(Carefully, seeing his time was near)
Through the gates and into the city.
They needed a steady old beast like me,
The noise was so great, and the flapping of palms.

When he left me he rubbed his hand
Across my shoulders and down my spine.
You will sire one more foal, he said
– Out of time for a beast, but think of Abraham –
And your line will bear my sign for ever
Across shoulders and back. Then blessing,
    he touched me,
And turned and went, on into the city's heart.

And will he return once more?
I should like to see him again.
One day . . .

O Lord, may I too, this Palm Sunday, know who you are, and the wonder. Help me to follow you into the city, and walk with you faithfully through all the week to come. And in the darkest hours, Lord, may I cling with faith to your promise that one day I shall see you again. And know the wonder. Amen.

Holy Monday

A meditation for the Church, on the parable of the Prodigal Son.

'Big Brother'

... But he was voted off!
He got it all wrong, and when finally
He showed himself a loser, then there was no question,
Out he went.
So how come I find him here, at the centre of attention,
New clothes, new rings, all the ballyhoo of celebrity?
I said to my father, I said,
'But he's lost his place, he's voted out;
How should it be that he's there
When he knows on any count
He lost the vote?'
And my father said – he said –
And I can't somehow get my head round it –
'Son, *your* place is safe; he's not taking yours.
But yes, the rules read differently, and have done
For quite some time. Two thousand years, in fact.
And his place with us is my gift
Because in love I choose to give him what is mine
    to give:
The grace of acceptance.
And what is mine, dear son, is yours, beloved faithful
    child,
Elder brother to the wanderer.
So now I give to you my greatest gift of all,
The will to offer full-hearted, undeserved grace.
All that I have is yours: so take that too,

Add it to your faithful uprightness,
You who are absolute for good,
Be in your steady purity
As absolute for grace.'

And when I would not, could not, he wept,
As once he wept over my wretched brother.
And I do not, *do not* understand why . . .

O my Father God, help me face the 'Big Brother' that is in me: that judges self-righteously, that is so conscious of its own struggles 'to be good' that it shuts out that best gift of all, your unconditional love to all. Help me to accept your ultimate gift to me: God's grace *for other people*. So may I begin to share your deepest joy, and so become a little more like your Son, my Lord Jesus Christ. Amen.

Holy Tuesday

Isaac

It taught me to ask questions about love, you see:
Since it was stranger, more mysterious
Than I had thought. Like death and life
Somehow mingled.
When we climbed the mountain, he and I
– It was strange even then, because
He had never had this look before
When we made sacrifice at home –
But as we climbed, his face was set like flint,
Remote, as though his whole will
Was narrowed to the point
Of a sharp knife.
I wanted him back, my father, so I said,
'My father' – wanting to ask –
And his voice seemed quite normal, his usual,
'Here I am, my son.'
So I asked the obvious: 'Where is the lamb
We must kill for the sacrifice?'
He looked at me then, and came back to me,
My father as I knew him; and he said,
'God himself will provide, my son.'
Then he looked somehow – shining – I don't know how
    to put it.
So we walked on, he and I, together now.

And He did, of course. God, I mean.
I had not struggled when my father bound me
And laid me on the altar.
You see, he looked – not angry, but – *loving* –

Yes, that's it, 'loving' . . .
So it all seemed dream-like, and God told me not to
   struggle.
So I did not struggle then: or ever again
(No hardship all my life:
An old woman's child, tenderly reared).
Woman's love: that I understood: that was my deepest
   safety.
First Sara, my mother, then Rebekah, my love, my wife.
But out in the world of faith and politics
Of sacrificial mountains and war over other men's wells,
I had no sure footing. For me the fields at evening in
   their peace.
Always I withdrew from conflict: God had taught me
Not to struggle . . .
My father now, he walked sure
Propelled by some knowledge, some inner dialogue
With the Jehovah I feared, God of the fire and knife.
But the Lord who gave my shamed, barren, ageing
   mother
A child; who brought my love Rebekah for me across
   the fields
At evening as I walked, and saw her and we loved;
That was the Lord I knew, that was the Lord
'Jehovah-jireh, the Lord who provides'.
So as I grow old now, and reflect on this
I do not understand how it can be
That it was on the terrible mountain of fire and
   upraised knife
That first my father taught me
'Jehovah-jireh, the Lord who provides'.
Can He be the same God who gave such tenderness
Through Sara and Rebekah in my loneliness?

I do not understand: a God for whom love
Means readiness to sacrifice an only son,
Who yet is so tender that my mother knew joy;
Who sent my love, my Rebekah, across the fields to me?
What Love is this which is both?
O Lord God of judgement, altar fire and knife,
And tender gentleness supplying all our needs,
Show us, show us, how these two loves merge.
Come to us, Lord God, and show us
That Love which is complete and wholly wills our
    good . . .
That Love which holds the sharp reality
Of fire and knife in human life,
And sacrifice and judgement on our waywardness,
And awe, and fear;
Holds them somehow within a goodness full of grace
Whose purposes for us, wholly benign,
Speak with a human voice that we can hear.
Recognize, like sheep their shepherd, and follow
    trustingly,
Knowing that He will guide,
Protect, nurture, carry and save.
Come to us, Lord God, in person showing us
That Love which wholly wills our good.

My father said He promised . . . it is strange . . .

O Love which is complete and wholly wills our good, our poor
little human understandings struggle to grasp even that you exist;
and seeing as you see is beyond us. But give us, like Isaac, glimpses
of what that completeness may be like – as we touch it with
wonder in Jesus; and for the rest, keep us trusting. Amen.

Holy Wednesday

A Holy Week meditation on Nebuchadnezzar

And King Nebuchadnezzar said 'Is not this great Babylon, which I have built by my mighty power for the glory of my majesty?' . . . Immediately he was driven from among men, his dwelling was with the beasts of the field, and he ate grass like an ox, and his body was wet with the dew of heaven, till seven times passed over him, till his hair grew as long as eagles' feathers and his nails were like birds' claws: until he should learn that the Most High rules the kingdom of men, and gives it to whom he will.

(verses from Daniel 4, adapted from the RSV)

The ox said:
(Wondering at this distorted creature)
'Strength? power?
You revel in strength?
I'm strong.
Power under orders,
Strong to pull and carry
Things others want moved.
I don't, myself, go for violence,
Not predatory, even to eat.
(I like the sweet grass, if you must know,
And even the great elephant is vegetarian.)
So my strength is for patience,
My power for enduring.
And obeying
His will.'
(. . . *and the king ate grass like an ox . . . his dwelling
was with the beasts of the field*)

The beasts said:
(Shading his body from the heat with their bulk,
And blowing warmly on his chilled flesh at night)
'In the night's chill think of the day's heat,
In the burning noon be glad, be glad, remembering
The cool dews of heaven;
So, unsheltered, sleep amid our shelter.'
Unpalaced, he learned
To be unhoused; but finding
In the creatures
(With whom he properly belonged)
The mute and mutual support
Of creatureliness.
Poor bare fork'd animal that he was,
Lear-like his pomp took physic;
And through his fellow creatures,
And with and among his fellow creatures
Learned to seek his meat – and fate – from God.
(. . . *and his body was wet with the dew of heaven.*)

The eagle said:
'In the flash of an eye
You see the world.
In the airy height
You are poised,
High. High.
Then you clasp with tightening claw
The crag in the sky.
Does not your height
But take you closer to God,
More open to his sight?
So know these lands
Circling beneath your eye

Are ours to roam by God's gift,
Not ours by right.'
(. . . *his hair grew as long as eagles' feathers, and his nails*
were like birds' claws.)

(. . . *till seven times passed over him*)
First: Rage.
Ejected from his kingdom. His!
Second: Fear.
The gauge
Of gathering terror.
Not kingship now,
But life itself. How
Survive, survive?
Third: Blankness.
Stupid with effort.
At this stage
Thought not possible.
Only survive.
Fourth: Tentative,
A flickering hope;
The beginnings of balance?
Slowly; finding oneself alive,
Wondering.
Fifth: A sort of fellowship,
A beginning of understanding
(From the creatures)
Of creatureliness.
Sixth: A trickle of delight
In the world he shared, and the God
Under whom he shared it.
Seventh: Discovery!
Blossoming into blessing, joy

In the Most High,
With his fellow creatures, the eagle in the height
And the ox in the field,
Under the dews from heaven.
(*At the end of the days, I Nebuchadnezzar lifted my eyes
to heaven, and my reason returned to me, and I blessed
the Most High and praised and honoured him.*)

Even so, Lord God,
In the pride of our technology
And our self-glorifying powers,
Return us as needful to our place,
Our creaturely place,
That our reason may return
And we may know once more
From whose hand
We hold our powers,
All we have and are:

And so learn blessing. Amen.

Maundy Thursday 1

> Peter, who did not remember,
> Denied his God,
> Yet after one serious glance
> Wept bitterly:
> Jesus, also glance at me
> When I will not repent:
> When I have done ill
> Stir my conscience.[71]

Lord, I know that not all is well with my soul, but like a minor disease I don't want to take too seriously, I don't actually look at it very much. It needs your glance, Lord: your *serious* glance. And then I look back at my course, and at my hidden heart's musings, and know them as other than you would have.

So now I lay them out before you, Lord. And I am sorry, sorry, sorry for what I see there. For all that is mean-spirited and ungenerous: for you, Lord, were – are – generous beyond conceiving. For all that is judgemental and unforgiving: for you, Lord, even agonizing on the Cross, continued not just your forgiving of the whole world, but with that last burst of particular personal forgiveness forgave the dying thief. And in that *particularity* I know that you include each unique soul that looks to you with penitently longing eyes: so I know that you include me, as I look at you this moment, knowing myself mortal, and under judgement, and yet defended by ultimate grace – your grace.

So may I live my life towards others today as one who knows what it is to deserve judgement and receive grace: may I in my thinking and my inner life, my words and my outer life, my actions and my relationships see others as indeed standing under judgement but rescued by your grace. And help me co-operate with that grace, Lord, not only in my own life but in assisting and liberating it in all with whom I have contact. Lord, they are your loved ones for whom you died: whether they wish me well or ill, bless them, forgive them, lead them, inspire them. And God be merciful to me, a sinner. Amen.

Maundy Thursday 2

It wasn't me
it was that woman
she doesn't know what's good
   for her
she did it

and then
it was that snake
I wouldn't have believed a word
I wouldn't have been taken in
imagine a talking snake
well I ask you

and then
and then
it was *you*
you gave me Eve
you made the serpent
it's your rotten apple
you know all about it
I was miles away
doing the garden like
   I was told
you're the one
you did it
it wasn't me
it *wasn't me*

And anyway I only took a little bite.[72]

O Lord, I'm wriggling like that wretched snake. I'm trying to wriggle out of accountability, Lord, and not just now . . . I find I justify myself, not only to myself and others, but to you. Lord God, there's often a lot of bluster in my prayers.

So help me today, Lord, to face truthfully whatever wrongs there are in my life. Help me to bring them to you penitently, asking your forgiveness. Heal me of the wounds that lie behind them; then strengthen me to do whatever can be done to set things right. Through *your* grace, Lord.

Only through your grace. Amen.

Good Friday

Pietà

And Mary, Lord? What of Mary?

It was just thirty-three years later
They all assembled for the second time;
(The soldiers had been late on the first occasion
– Too late).
But they were here in numbers now.
And when due time was come
His bed was ready; two planks of wood
Well-padded with softest hay, that first time.
Two planks of wood this last time too,
Rough and bare, on which he stretched out,
Readily, though pillowless, unswaddled,
Surrendering himself to that last sleep.

The countryfolk came again
Drawn by a drama whose nature mystified them
('And the people who stood beholding'
– did not depart glorifying God).
'Wise' men there too, had made an inner journey
To reach this place, informed by sacred knowledge,
Too narrow a knowledge, so their gift to him was death.
There were even some oxen, hauling wood nearby,
And a laden donkey, whose home-bound master
Paused with his beast to see
What thing this might be which had come to pass.
And Mary? Always God the Father had sent
To support her through the huge crises of her calling
A sturdy man, to cherish and protect:

That first time Joseph, this time John,
(She had other sons in plenty, but his appointment was
    divine).
And now her hour was almost come.
Instead of blazing light across the heavens
Black darkness fell at noon:
No angel song, but trembling of the earth.
And Mary knew the birthpangs once again
But could not know the new Creation
Coming that agonizing moment
Into life.
She only knew that at the last
She would gather up her child again
(Bloodied as at that first far-off birthing).
One last time she would gather him up
And cradle him within her arms.
And could she glimpse through all that blinding pain
That this too,

This too, was Heaven's gift?

O Lord, this Good Friday, help me to stand alongside Mary in
whatever guise she appears in our world. For the sake of what
you did on the Cross. Amen.

The ballad of the Judas Tree

In Hell there grew a Judas Tree
Where Judas hanged and died,
Because he could not bear to see
His master crucified.

Our Lord descended into Hell
And found his Judas there,
Forever hanging from the tree
Grown from his own despair.

So Jesus cut his Judas down
And took him in his arm:
'It was for this I came,' he said
'And not to do you harm.

My Father gave me twelve good men
And all of them I've kept
Though one betrayed and one denied
Some fled and others slept.

In three days' time I shall return
To make the others glad
But first I had to come to Hell
And share the death you had.

My Tree will grow in place of yours
Its roots strike here as well.
There is no final victory
Without this soul from Hell.'

So when we all condemn him
As of every traitor worst

Remember that of all his men
Our Lord forgave him first.

Lord, you were prepared to go to the uttermost depths to rescue us: even our self-made depths. We all have them, Lord. We've all been there, with Peter in his denial and Judas in his betrayal and those 'who all forsook him and fled . . .'

Your journey between Good Friday and Easter Sunday is a mystery beyond us. I only know that you did it for us all, with no exceptions except self-chosen ones.

So don't, in this solemn moment, let *me* start making exceptions. Keep me out of that seat of judgement that is yours, not mine. Instead, let me be with Peter and all those others listening to your words of total forgiveness. For that is resurrection. For that is a resurrection we can know this very day. Help me receive it, Lord. Amen.

Christ harrows hell

And from the heart
of light
A loud voice spoke
Open
These gates, Lucifer,
Prince of this land; the King of glory,
A crown upon his head
Comes . . .

Dukes of this dark place
Undo these gates so that Christ come
In, the Son of heaven's King.
With that word, Hell split apart,
Burst its devil's bars; no man
Nor guard could stop the gates swing
Wide . . .
The people who had walked
In darkness, 'Behold the Lamb
Of God', with John sang now.
And Lucifer could not look
At it, the light blinding him.
And along that light all those
Our Lord loved came streaming out.[73]

(*Based on the apocryphal story of Christ's release of those imprisoned in hell – 'harrow' in Middle English means 'to rob' – when he descended into hell after the crucifixion and before the resurrection.*)

O my Lord and my God, Christ victorious, as I look expectantly for Easter's dawning, I pray for all those sunk this day in different sorts of hell. Those shut up in despair, those locked in incurable disease and pain, those caged in their own anger against you and/or the world, those padlocked in inconsolable grief. Harrow their hell for them this night, Lord, and bring them out in the steady stream of your light. Those whose deeds and attitudes imprison them; the cruel, the greedy, the power-hungry, the predatory: O unstoppable light, search out their prisons, break the bars of sin, and bring them through to a world made holy.

Lord Jesus, I ask this, with deep thankfulness this Eastertide that you rescued *me*, and brought me out of life's ambiguous prison, and set my feet in your way of freedom.

Glory be to you. Glory be to you. Glory be to you. Amen.

Easter Sunday

Easter hymn

Death and darkness, get you packing,
Nothing now to man is lacking,
All your triumphs now are ended,
And what Adam marred is mended; . . .
Then unto him, who thus hath thrown
Even to contempt, thy kingdom down,
And by thy blood did us advance
Unto his own inheritance,
To him be glory, power, praise
From thee, unto the last of days.[74]

Easter St John

God so loved he gave
God loved so he gave
God loved, he gave so

So teach me to love
So I may love, I'll give
So I may give, I'll love
I may so love to give.

Teach me Lord sto give,
And giving love, and loving give

So Thou be gift and love so.

O Love that defeated darkness and death, for
all humanity, for all Creation . . .

And for me;
In awed astonishment I gaze at you.
Can death truly die?

O loving Lord and radiant Lord, let me, this twenty-first-century day, in wondering joy enter again into our Easter inheritance, and claim for this world and all that it inhabit, the end of despair, and the certainties of new life. And in that faith, Lord, make me ever more loving and giving, with the love that is your gift and our guarantor. Amen.

For Easter Day

A prayer for the gathered community

In the power of the Spirit and in union with Christ, let us pray
to the Father:

'Rejoice and be glad, Mother Church! and let your holy
courts in radiant light resound with the praise of your
people', for:

On this glorious day . . . the tomb was empty and our
Lord alive, his risen glory proclaimed by angels and seen
by men and women. Lord Christ, help us, your Church,
to rise by this same power from all that would entomb *us*,
in confidence and joy to be the living body of Christ
serving in the world today.

God of resurrection: hear our prayer.

On this glorious day . . . the disciples for fear were hidden
behind locked doors, and you came to them and
transformed their fear into unshakeable trust and joy. May
all today's isolated or persecuted Christians find fresh
strength and hope in the good news of Easter.

God of resurrection: hear our prayer.

On this glorious day . . . there were those who grieved
because they had hoped the nation would be restored to
political power. And you walked with them and so showed
them your way of true life for the world that their hearts
burned within them. Lord Christ, may today's world
leaders so learn to walk with you that their understandings
are transformed, and they learn to work together to end

war and assuage homelessness and famine; that the
nations may know themselves redeemed and blessed.

God of resurrection: hear our prayer.

On this glorious day . . . your followers and friends were
beset by guilt as well as grief: they had fled, had denied.
Yet you, Lord, came to *all* in your risen power, even to
those who doubted. So come this Easter into our
communities and our homes, teaching us by your own
forgiving and life-giving love to forgive each other, to be
faithful, and to serve you in each other and in those
among whom we live.

God of resurrection: hear our prayer.

On this glorious day . . . Mary Magdalene came to the
tomb in desolation, seeking comfort only in last services
to the dead. In her grief you came to her and called her
by name. Be a living presence in the same way to all those
who today suffer the terrible anguish of loss, or are in
pain, fear, bewilderment, anxiety or desolation. May they
too hear you call them by name, and in this Eastertide
know comfort and a new and living hope.

God of resurrection: hear our prayer.

On this glorious day . . . the stone was rolled away and the
grave-clothes discarded. We remember now all those who
have died trusting in God's grace. And we pray that this
same power that moved the stone and brought our Lord
Jesus Christ from the grave, may give us, with them, a part
in his victory over death, and in his risen life, for ever.

*Merciful Father, accept these prayers
for the sake of your Son, our Saviour, Jesus Christ.
Amen.*

Eastertide 1

So proclaim it in the high rise,
in the hostel let it ring;
make it known in Cardboard City,
let the homeless rise and sing:
'He is Lord of life abundant
and he changes everything;
the Lord is risen indeed.'[75]

'And he changes everything . . .' Lord of resurrection, if we do not take your new life into the high-rise and the hostel then we have not taken it into our own hearts. If your new life does not surge through Cardboard City, proclaimed by our own engagement there, then that new life does not dwell in our own homes. If we do not give the homeless cause to know that Easter changes everything, then Easter has not changed what most needs changing in our own lives.

So, my risen Lord, I turn from the joyous celebrations in churches and chapels and in your shining and risen presence ask:

Have *I* this Easter given anyone in hostel, high-rise, Cardboard City, grey tenements, sleazy suburbs, cause to say with wonder, 'But Christ changes everything!'

If I have not, Lord, why not? And what, today, am I going to do about it?

Have *I* this Easter given any homeless cause to leap to their weary feet and sing out in astonishment, 'Here is one who changes everything!'

If I have not, Lord, why not? And what, today, am I going to do about it?

Lord, often it's so difficult to know what I *can* do. But I can make a start. I can start by believing that Easter is indeed a message of transformation for the desolate urban places and those who live in them, and that I have my part to play in making resurrection things happen. I can use my voice and my skills to struggle for justice and generosity for the no-hopers. I can stand up when it's unpopular for the minorities and the unwanted immigrants. Even more simply, I can talk to the *Big Issue* sellers as well as buying from them; I can connect with the lad curled up in his sleeping bag with that small dog in the shop doorway, and hear his story as well as buying him (and the dog) a pie. And containing my instinctive timidity, and accepting rejection if it comes, I can see you, my crucified Lord, standing in risen power behind every derelict figure I speak to as a fellow human being.

Lord of high-rise and hostel, of the homeless and marginalized, of the threatening urban territories of the angry and the failing, teach me, O my dear Lord teach me, that Easter changes everything or it changes nothing, and so it must begin – and continue – by changing *me*. So let me live out the power of Easter in this very place, Lord. Never doubting that here, even here, you intend life abundant: and it is for me, in your strength, to help make it happen. Amen. Amen.

Eastertide 2

(*And he upbraided them for their unbelief . . .*)

> Make no mistake
> if he rose at all
> it was as his body;
> if the cells' dissolution did not reverse,
>   the molecules re-knit, the amino acids rekindle,
>   the church will fall . . .
>
> Let us not mock God with metaphor,
> analogy, side-stepping transcendence;
> making of the event a parable, a sign painted
>   in the faded credulity of earlier ages;
> let us walk through the door.
>
> The stone is rolled back, not papier maché,
> not a stone in a story,
> but the vast rock of materiality that in the slow
>   grinding of time will eclipse in each of us
> the wide light of day . . .
> Let us not seek to make it less monstrous,
> for our own convenience, our own sense of beauty,
> lest, awakened in one unthinkable hour, we
>   are embarrassed by the miracle,
> and crushed by remonstrance.[76]

It is not within the nature of dry bones to live again.

> Son of man, can these bones live? And I answered, O Lord
> GOD, thou knowest.
>
> (*Ezekiel 37.3, AV*)

It is not within the nature of a dead body to be restored to life. O, my Lord, it is not within the nature of being betrayed to give one's life for the one betraying. It is not within the nature of the divine to put on human finitude. It is not within the nature of absolute authority to put on human vulnerability. It is not within the nature of absolute justice to put on absolute mercy.

Yet all these things – O my Lord and my God! – have happened in our human history, where in you, my Lord Christ, the glory of God's transcendence transformed it; where eternity has crossed time and transfigured it.[77]

> My gracious Master and my God
> Assist me to proclaim,
> To spread through all the earth abroad
> The wonders of thy name.[78]

Amen: O, in the light of Easter, Amen.

Eastertide 3

and that will be heaven
at last   the first unclouded
seeing
        to stand like the sunflower
turned full face to the sun   drenched
with light   in the still centre
held   while the circling planets
hum with an utter joy

                seeing and knowing
at last   in every particle
seen and known   and not turning away
        never turning away[79]

When she died and had gone to be with you, Father, I wanted
so desperately to go too. It was not simply that the world was
such a grey and empty place at this time of loss – though it
was, and it seemed as though never would it be bright and full
of life again. But it was more than that. When we make the journey right to the very gate of Heaven itself, with someone we
love; and then they must go on and we must go back . . . Then,
O my Father, we get a glimpse, just a glimpse, of the radiant
reality of the world beyond, the bright eternity promised. And
we long for it, like a child glimpsing home through the gates
and suddenly recognizing this is where we belong.

Slowly, the wounds heal. Slowly, life and colour come back
to the world. The bright focus of things beyond slowly fades,
and with it the intense truth of what lies ahead for us.

Father God, I know this must happen, and that after the
glimpse of the celestial we must come down from the trans-

figured mountain of fire and live out the rest of the life that is meant for your service. But do not take away from us, Father, that hunger for home. I do not want it healed. I want it to remain for me as a promise – Christ's Easter promise: a knowledge deep within me that there will be that first unclouded seeing; that gentle warmth of drenching light; that still serenity; that circling of joy. And seeing and knowing, seen and known, utterly and wholly, I shall never be turned away from loved ones again. Never turn away from you, my Lord . . .

O my Lord Jesus: keep this Easter hope alive and true in my heart. Always. Amen.

Eastertide 4

O death, where is thy sting?

'Come out of jail, Mary,' he said, 'the doors are open
    And joy has its ear cocked for your coming.
Earth is no place to mope in. So throw away
Your doubt, cast every clout of care,
Hang all your hallelujahs out
This airy day' . . .[80]

'Cast every clout of care' . . . O my dear Lord, all our instinct is against it! 'Ne'er cast a clout till May be out' – and whether it's the month or the blossom we're talking of, it still means 'caution!' Don't assume this sunshine warmth is here to stay just because it feels like it. Cold airs have a way of returning and blighting us in our joyous summer apparel, along with the early blossoming flowers. Isn't that the truth of it, Lord, here in this northern land?

And just as for the year's seasons, so for our spiritual seasons. We wrap ourselves up against the soul's cold, we treat cautiously those early flags of summer, the dapples of spring sunshine in our soul. Don't count on it, we say to ourselves.

But we're wrong this time, Lord. And we need your loving challenge to the way we cling to our soul's defences. For Earth is now no place to mope in: *and never will be again* . . . O dear Lord, forgive us that we so rarely live and think and judge life as your Easter people. O dear Lord, forgive *me* that I so often let today's darkness cloud the radiance of your eternal day. Your bright day, which began for us on Easter morning and has never since ceased, and awaits, awaits, awaits our daily recognition with rejoicing. *O good morning, my Lord and my God: for ever, good morning!*

Sometimes on a bright day I wear sunglasses for the radiance is so intense. And I forget when I come in from the sunshine of God's wide world to my room inside, where I have things to struggle with, that I'm wearing them. And the room looks intensely dark. And my spirits drop. Until suddenly I remember, and remove them; I glance out of the window at the bright day, and then turn to my room again, and lo! it too is bright, even in its shadowed places, with the reflected glory of the day; your day . . .

So today – and each day, Lord – help me to remove whatever darkens my gaze. Today – and each day, Lord – help me throw away my doubts. Today – and each day, Lord – help me cast my clout of care, and recall that I belong to an Easter people, all the time, everywhere.

And may the hallelujahs I hang out be such as raise hope in the hopeless, new certainty in the doubting, and gladness in those for whom joy has been frosted over. For love of my risen Lord. Amen.

Eastertide 5

An alternative ending to St Mark's Gospel

Later he appeared to the eleven themselves as they were sitting at the table; and he upbraided them for their lack of faith and stubbornness, because they had not believed those who saw him after he had risen. And they excused themselves, saying, 'This age of lawlessness is under Satan, who does not allow the truth and power of God to prevail over the unclean things of the spirits. Therefore reveal your righteousness now' – thus they spoke to Christ. And Christ replied unto them, 'The term of years of Satan's power has been fulfilled, but other terrible things draw near. And for those who have sinned I was handed over to death, that they may return to the truth and sin no more.'

(Mark 16)

Lord, this mysterious ending to St Mark's Gospel challenges me very strongly. For so often it feels as though we, your people of the twenty-first century, are like that original 'eleven' in the aftermath of the events of Holy Week and Easter. Seated round the table, they seem caught, like us, between the extraordinary power of the astonishing and transformative experiences they have lived through or been told of, and the sheer weight of a world around them not only disbelieving but seemingly quite unchanged, still 'an age of lawlessness under Satan'. So that, *knowing* life is changed for ever, somehow they can't move into living out that knowledge.

Lord, looking around now at my world, that is still often how it seems. Still it feels to be 'an age of lawlessness under Satan'.

So, like these early apostles, we turn to you and say, 'Reveal your righteousness *now*'. After the wonder of celebrating Easter, we quickly lose our sense that Easter is now, and always, whatever the time of year. That your righteousness has indeed already been revealed, once and for all, and still runs and is at work among us daily, if we will but see: and to see, we have only to look. And its power is continuous. *And I have known it, Lord.*

So we – I – need to hear you again, declaring to us that the power of evil is broken, its time done. And that though 'terrible things draw near' – as they have continued to do in the last 2,000 years – yet I face them, like all your people since that first mind-blowing Easter day, in the power of what you have done to free us, all of us, that 'we might return to truth and sin no more'. Sin: the conducting of one's life as though it is not under the sovereignty of God.

So, my Lord Christ, I bring to you all that in me and my church is aligned with the dithering of those disciples, as I glimpse them here on the edge of a full commitment to living in the power – the wonderful, crazy, life-transforming power – of the Easter gospel. Dear Lord, help me and all your people to stop dithering on the edge of life-change, and, as these same apostles were to do so wholeheartedly, go out into your world declaring by our lives the coming of the kingdom of Heaven. Starting with an act of faith *now*, Lord, that will stay with me when I rise and go from this place:

> So now I tell the secret
> that resurrection is the glass
> through which we see things differently,
> and what was first in the mind of God
> becomes the truth at last.[81]

Amen, Lord: so be it.

Ascension Day

To complete your seamless robe, and so to complete our
faith, you ascended through the air into the heavens,
before the very eyes of the apostles. In this way you
showed that you are the Lord of all, and are the very
fulfilment of all creation. Thus from that moment every
human and every living creature should bow at your
name. And, in the eyes of faith, we can see that all
creation proclaims your greatness.[82]

My Lord Jesus Christ, I do not really begin to understand the
mystery of your Ascension, or how to picture it. Only I know
there had to be a time when your physical presence must be
withdrawn, for our faith to become more mature, not depend-
ent on such props to belief as those first sightings. And because
the wider world must encounter the immediacy of your love
as vitally as your first disciples had, through whatever channels
you would use in the centuries that lay ahead. And I know
that my tender and suffering Lord, and even my victoriously
risen and observable Lord, must become the aweful and glorious
Lord, King beyond time and space, ruling over all the worlds
that are and that are to be. And I understand that at your Ascension you went through the door between time and eternity
in a new and significant way.

Only, Lord, I should be full of a sense of loss, if it were not
for being with your disciples as they return to Jerusalem, not
sad but full of a great joy, bursting into hymns praising God.
Lord, it seems that they do not so much see you leaving them,
as taking up your rule over all the unacknowledged bits of
their lives, including their fears and hopes for eternity. They

show such a profound sense of wondering certainty, Lord, an absoluteness of commitment, devotion and worship.

So, Lord, I return with them to the city. In me also take up your rule over all the unacknowledged bits of my being; fill me too with awe and praise as you take up your kingly rule over everything that is. And renew within me the wonder of Ascension Day discipleship. Amen.

Pentecost

Now the earth was formless and empty, darkness was
over the surface of the deep, and the Spirit of God was
hovering over the waters.

(Genesis 1.2, NIV)

Suddenly a sound like the blowing of a violent wind came
from heaven and filled the whole house where they were
sitting. They saw what seemed to be tongues of fire that
separated and came to rest on each of them. All of them
were filled with the Holy Spirit and began to speak in
other tongues.

(Acts 2.2–4, NIV)

O surging Spirit, mighty wind of God, blow through my heart
today. Let me not fear your energy and force, but welcome it
in my life. Let it disperse all those accretions, those patterns of
life and worship I have come to rely on and take pleasure in
for their own sake rather than as ways to you. Disturb my
complacencies, Lord, the things I cling to for security in place
of clinging to you. And in their place give me the wonder of
your fire, of God's holy flames above my head and in my heart.

O gentle Spirit, breathing on the face of the waters in those
depths of my heart still unformed and in darkness; in that
deepest part of me where there is still chaos, shape your order
and harmony, bring forth your design in new life.

O creator Spirit, may I be part of your creative life in the
world. Help me, like your first disciples, take its wonder out into
my world; and enable me to reject all that within me is destructive or malign or repressive. Let me rejoice selflessly in your
creative work in others, glorying in the wonders of God in
other people's lives. And bond us together in the life and call-

ing of the Church, whose birth we celebrate today, born after the terrors of the Cross and the marvels of the Resurrection, born by your will in the fire and wind of the Spirit's coming. Keep us, your people of today, aflame with your new life for the whole creation, in the love and power of the triune God, Father, Son and Holy Spirit. Amen.

Trinity Sunday

May none of God's wonderful works
   Keep silence, night or morning.
Bright stars, high mountains, the depths of the seas,
   Sources of rushing rivers:
May all these break into song, as we sing
   To Father, Son and Holy Spirit.
May all the angels in the heavens reply:
   Amen! Amen! Amen!
Power, praise, honour, eternal glory
   To God, the only Giver of grace.
   Amen! Amen! Amen![83]

Today, my living, loving, holy God, today my prayer is entirely and explicitly in your praise. Not about my needs and hopes and wants, not even those of my world. This special day is one to revel in your praise. For you have helped us glimpse – only glimpse – the mystery of how complete is the Godhead, needing no other beyond itself. And yet you chose to reach out to humanity, and with humanity all creation, all the spinning universes so far beyond our measuring. And all the hosts of Heaven, those beings of whom we know rumours, whose agency we glimpse occasionally going about your bidding. O holy God, I reflect with awe that all things praise you, and that you have created us thus.

And small and insignificant as I am, Lord God, in the presence of your aweful holiness, yet I too can offer my praise:

  — for the wonder and mystery of your being, Father, Son and Holy Spirit.

— for the wonder and mystery of your relationship with your creation, seen and unseen.

— for the wonder and mystery of your design for us.

O God, whose nature and way of being is that of love, I reflect with joy on the wonder that you love and know the whole vastness of your creation, in its smallest detail, from sparrow to mighty planet.

And small and insignificant as I am, Lord God, in the presence of that inconceivable love, yet I too can offer my praise:

> Praise to the holiest in the height,
> and in the depth be praise;
> In all his works most wonderful,
> most sure in all his ways.[84]

Amen.

Finally . . .

The fullness of time

On a rusty iron throne
Past the furthest star of space
I saw Satan sit alone,
Old and haggard was his face;
For his work was done and he
Rested in eternity.

And to him from out the sun
Came his father and his friend
Saying, now the work is done
Enmity is at an end:
And he guided Satan to
Paradises that he knew.

Gabriel without a frown,
Uriel without a spear,
Raphael came singing down
Welcoming their ancient peer,
And they seated him beside
One that had been crucified.[85]

O my astonishingly risen Lord, as Easter Day and the Easter season slips behind me with its intense and wondering joy, the world around me has re-entered 'ordinary time' in its mind-set and preoccupations. And it is not easy to avoid going with that world and myself leaving the life-changing truth of Easter behind.

So I want today to reclaim Eastertide for my everyday life, Lord; since all time is now resurrection time and every season is Easter. For because of your victory over our sick destructiveness and our very mortality itself, *we are entered into the beginning of the fullness of time.* All unaware, we are, your Creation, part of its mighty movement towards completion, when all your resurrection work shall be done, all enmity shall be at an end, and we shall see, with understanding at last, in your unveiled presence, our redeemed Paradise.

O my dear and victorious Lord, help me to take the truth of that into the very deep of my soul, and live my ordinary daily life shaped by it. And for those who all over the world are at this moment experiencing only the blackest of Good Fridays, I ask that the same power with which you overcame may surround them, protect them, comfort and strengthen them, and a whisper of victory, even there in their terrible place, be theirs. Especially I pray for those known to me, and I name them here _____

May everything I do and am, and my life with others each day, grow from that glorious certainty of Love triumphant and for ever. Because of Easter. Amen.

Envoi

Traditional blessing from Durham Cathedral on St Cuthbert's Day

Go in peace, with God to enfold you:
God in your speaking,
God in your thinking,
God in your sleeping,
God in your waking,
God in your watching,
God in your hoping;
God in your life,
God on your lips,
God in your heart,
and God in your eternity.

Amen.[86]

Notes

All material not otherwise designated is by Ruth Etchells.

1. Anne Ridler, from 'Open House', in *Cathedrals*, Winchester College Printing Society, 1979.
2. Anatoli Levitin, in *Miracle of Prayer*, Keston College, quoted in *The Lion Prayer Collection*, compiled by Mary Batchelor, Lion, 1992, 1998.
3. Gerard Kelly, 'The Very Thought of Thee', in *The Lion Christian Poetry Collection*, compiled by Mary Batchelor, Lion, 1995.
4. John Ormond, from 'Cathedral Builders', in *Cathedrals*, see note 1.
5. Kathy Galloway, from 'God beyond borders', in *Maker's Blessing*, Wild Goose Publications, 1999, http://www.ionabooks.com
6. Adapted from Dag Hammarskjöld, from *Markings*, trans. W. H. Auden and Leif Sjöberg, Faber and Faber, 1964; quoted in *CMS Prayerletter*, 1999.
7. C. S. Lewis, in *The Hodder Book of Prayers in Large Print*, ed. Rosemary Curtis, Hodder and Stoughton, 1997. Reproduced by permission of The C. S. Lewis Company Ltd.
8. Joseph Addison, in *Hymns Ancient and Modern, New Standard*, Lambeth Conference Gift Edition, 1998.
9. The General Thanksgiving from the Church of England Book of Common Prayer, 1662. Extracts from The Book of Common Prayer, the rights in which are vested in the Crown, are reproduced by permission of the Crown's Patentee, Cambridge University Press.

10. From *Celtic Fire: An Anthology of Celtic Christian Literature* (prayers *c.* AD 450–700), ed. R. Van de Weyer, Darton, Longman and Todd, 1990.

11. Elizabeth Jennings, from 'Into the Hour', in 'Moments of Grace', *Collected Poems*, Carcanet, 1986. Reproduced by permission of David Higham Associates Ltd.

12. John Masefield, from 'Saul Kane's Conversion', in 'The Everlasting Mercy', *Collected Poems*, Heinemann, 1929. Reproduced by permission of the Society of Authors as the Literary Representative of the Estate of John Masefield.

13. Miguel de Guavera, 'Sonnet', trans. Samuel Beckett, from *An Anthology of Mexican Poetry*, Thames and Hudson, 1959.

14. Anne Bradstreet, from 'Meditations Divine and Moral', in *The New Oxford Book of English Prose*, ed. John Gross, Oxford University Press, 1998.

15. Michelangelo, Sonnet LXVII, trans. Elizabeth Jennings, in 'Sonnets of Michelangelo', *Collected Poems*, see note 11. Reproduced by permission of David Higham Associates Ltd.

16. From *Morning, Noon and Night*, ed. John Carden, Church Missionary Society, 1976.

17. Kathy Galloway, from 'Monday: up against the wall', in *Love Burning Deep*, SPCK, 1993.

18. Anonymous Welsh, thirteenth century, in *A Deep But Dazzling Darkness*, ed. Lucy Lethbridge and Selina O'Grady, Darton, Longman and Todd, 2002.

19. W. B. Yeats, in *A Deep But Dazzling Darkness*, see note 18. Reproduced by permission of A. P. Watt on behalf of Michael B. Yeats.

20. Carmen Bernos de Gasztold, in *Prayers from the Ark*, trans. Rumer Godden, Macmillan, 1963.

21. Trans. from the Dutch by G. R. Woodward, in *The Oxford Book of Carols*, Oxford University Press, 1963.

22. Søren Kierkegaard, quoted in *A Prayer for Owen Meany*, John Irvine, Blackwood, 1989, p. 326.
23. Carmen Bernos de Gasztold, see note 20.
24. From a prayer card from Fairacres, published by SLG Press, Fairacres, Oxford. Reproduced by kind permission of SLG Press.
25. Fred Kaan, in *New Hymns and Worship Songs*, compiled by Kevin Mayhew, Kevin Mayhew Ltd, 2001. Copyright © 1989 Stainer & Bell Ltd, extract from 'The Only Earth We Knew'.
26. George MacDonald, from 'January' (slightly adapted), in *A Deep But Dazzling Darkness*, see note 18.
27. Ann Lewin, from 'Revelation', in *Watching for the King fisher*, Inspire Methodist Publishing House, 2004.
28. Anonymous prayer from Ravensbruck concentration camp, in *Blessings*, ed. Mary Craig, Hodder and Stoughton, 1979. Reprinted by permission of PFD on behalf of Mary Craig.
29. John Morris, from 'Providence', in *Contemporary Creed*, O Books, 2005. Quoted by Ruth Gledhill, *Church of England Newspaper*, 24 February 2006.
30. Richard Baxter, from 'Christ who knows all his sheep' (adapted), in *Hymns Ancient and Modern, New Standard*, see note 8.
31. Don Marquis, 'Waiting for the Echo', quoted by Cathy Fox, *Church of England Newspaper*, 22 April 2004.
32. William Langland, from *The Book Concerning Piers the Plowman*, trans. Donald Attwater, in *The New Oxford Book of Christian Verse*, ed. Donald Davie, Oxford University Press, 1981. Reproduced by permission of J. M. Dent & Sons, a division of The Orion Publishing Group.
33. John Bell and Graham Maule, Wild Goose Resource Group, Iona Community, 1987. Verses 1–3 of 5, words: John Bell and Graham Maule, copyright © 1987 WGRG, Iona Community, Glasgow G2 3DH.

34. William Langland, from *Visions from Piers Plowman*, rendered by Nevill Coghill, Dent and Sons Ltd, 1949, 1970. Reproduced by permission of J. M. Dent & Sons, a division of The Orion Publishing Group.

35. Albert Einstein, from 'The world as I see it', in *Something Understood*, compiled by Beverley McAinsh, Hodder and Stoughton, 2001.

36. Francis Bacon, 'To God the Father' (first published 1679), in *The New Oxford Book of English Prose*, see note 14.

37. From the prayer of St Columba of Iona, Irish missionary (521–97), quoted in *CMS Prayerletter*, November 1999.

38. Christopher Smart, from 'Jubilate Deo', in *Collected Poems*, ed. Norman Callan, Muses Library, Routledge, 1949.

39. Thomas Ken, in *Hymns Ancient and Modern, New Standard*, see note 8.

40. Ogden Nash, in *The Lion Prayer Collection*, see note 2. Copyright © 1961, 1962 by Ogden Nash. Reprinted by permission of Curtis Brown Ltd.

41. Timothy Dudley-Smith, in *New Hymns and Worship Songs*, see note 25. Text copyright Timothy Dudley-Smith in Europe (including UK and Ireland) and in all territories not controlled by the Hope Publishing Company, USA.

42. Adapted from the Roman Liturgy, in *A Treasury of Prayer*, compiled by Tony Castle, Hodder and Stoughton, 1983.

43. Edwina Gately, 'A Julian Contemplation', in *Something Understood*, see note 35.

44. Danielle O'Driscoll, from 'Middle Class Blues', *New and Selected Poems*, Anvil, 2005.

45. Ben Okri, from 'An African Elegy', *Poems*, Jonathan Cape, 1992 (read at his Booker Prize presentation).

46. Adapted by S. Dauermann, Lillenas Publishing Co., 1975, in *New Hymns and Worship Songs*, see note 25.

47. From The Litany, *Common Worship (Rogation Version)*, Church House Publishing, 2000.

48. William Langland, from 'Paradoxes of Salvation', in *Visions from Piers Plowman*, see note 34.

49. Corrie Ten Boom, in *Women of Prayer*, ed. Dorothy M. Stewart, Collins Fount, 1993.

50. From 'A Prayer of the Baralong', *CMS Prayerletter*, 22 February 1998.

51. William Cowper, 'God moves in a mysterious way' (*Olney Hymns*, 1779), *William Cowper: Selected Poems*, ed. Nick Rhodes, Carcanet Press, 1981.

52. Henry Martyn, reflecting on Matthew 9.20–22, *CMS Prayerletter*, 2 May 1999.

53. Neil Perry, in *A Touch of Flame*, ed. Jenny Robertson, Lion, 1989.

54. Esther de Waal, in *Seeking God*, Collins Fount, 1984.

55. Kathy Galloway, in *Talking to the Bones*, SPCK, 1996.

56. Philip Larkin, in *Collected Poems*, Faber and Faber, 2003.

57. Olivia Michael, in *New Christian Poetry*, Collins Flame, 1990.

58. R. S. Thomas, in *Experimenting with an Amen*, Macmillan, 1995.

59. Kathy Galloway, in *Love Burning Deep*, see note 17.

60. William Baldwin, in 'The Canticles and Ballads of Solomon' (1549), in *The New Oxford Book of Christian Verse*, see note 32.

61. Abd Ab' Azuz Al-Dirini, from 'Purity of Heart', in *Morning, Noon and Night*, see note 16.

62. J. H. Newman, in *The Oxford Book of Prayer*, ed. G. Appleton, Oxford University Press, 1985.

63. Nicolas Freeling, *Double Barrel*, Victor Gollancz, 1964, chapter 27.

64. F. W. Faber, from 'Souls of men why will you scatter?', *Hymns Ancient and Modern, New Standard*, see note 8.

65. Leslie Neeris, from 'At the sea's edge in Pembrokeshire' (speaking of Peter de Lera, builder of St David's Cathedral) in *Cathedrals*, see note 1.

66. Judith Sequeira, 'Focus on Christ' (adapted), *My Cross, God's Image*, vol. 10, no. 2, Summer 1991, with permission from the Asia Women's Resource Centre for Culture and Theology, Kuala Lumpur. In *The Hodder Book of Prayers in Large Print*, see note 7.

67. David Coleman, in *Maker's Blessing*, see note 5.

68. Philip Larkin, in *Collected Poems*, see note 56.

69. Rosalind Brown, 27 October 2000; copyright © Rosalind Brown: permission given for use here. Written for Remembrance Day, 11 November 2000. As a hymn set to the music, *Finlandia*.

70. Traditional Spiritual (adapted), in Ruth Etchells, *Just As I Am*, SPCK, 1994.

71. Christian Friedrich Henrici, aka 'Picador', from the libretto of Bach's *St Matthew Passion*, translator unknown.

72. Geoffrey Rust, 'Adam', in *A Touch of Flame*, see note 53.

73. William Langland, in *The Vision of Piers Plowman*, trans. Ronald Tamplin, in *The Sun, Dancing*, ed. Charles Causley, Kestrel, 1982.

74. Henry Vaughan, from 'Easter Hymn', *Selected Poems*, ed. Louis Martz, Oxford University Press, 1995.

75. Michael Forster, in *New Hymns and Worship Songs*, see note 25.

76. John Updike, from 'Seven Stanzas for Easter', *Collected Poems, 1953–93*, Hamish Hamilton, 1993.

77. Ruth Etchells, in *Set My People Free*, HarperCollins, 1995.

78. Charles Wesley, from 'O for a thousand tongues to sing', in *Hymns Ancient and Modern, New Standard*, see note 8.

79. Evangeline Paterson, in *The Lion Christian Poetry Collection*, see note 3. Reproduced by kind permission of Carolyn Resoland-Jones.

80. W. R. Rodgers, from 'Resurrection', in *Poems* (1993). By kind permission of the estate of W. R. Rodgers and The Gallery Press, Loughcrew, Oldcastle, Castlemeath, Ireland.

81. David Scott, from 'Resurrection', *Piecing Together*, Bloodaxe Books, 2005.

82. Bernard of Clairvaux, from *On the Christian Year*, trans. by a religious from the Community of St Mary the Virgin.

83. Egyptian doxology (third to sixth century), in *Early Christian Prayers*, ed. A. Hammam, Longman, 1961.

84. J. H. Newman, 'Praise to the holiest in the height', in *Hymns Ancient and Modern, New Standard*, see note 8.

85. James Stephens, in *The Sun, Dancing*, see note 73.

86. Traditional blessing on St Cuthbert's day in Durham Cathedral: source unknown.

Thematic Index

Author Index